PRAISE FOR *HOW TO WRITE EFFECTIVE BUSINESS ENGLISH*
THIRD EDITION

'If you need a handy toolkit for improving your business writing across media and generations, this practical guide is packed with advice, tips and examples to help you do just that.

It works for both native and non-native English speakers wishing to inject more vitality and clarity into their business writing. I recommend you keep it close to your computer or laptop – or in the office to help colleagues boost their writing skills. Dip into it when you need some inspiration.

As language evolves so too should our business writing skills if we wish to stay ahead of the competition. The author's #wordpowerskills system (in four easy-to-use steps), checklists and tips will ensure your writing leads to action, reaction and results. It will energize your business writing and your readers' experience.

I will definitely recommend this book to my students, especially the section on generational writing. It's not all WhatsApp and Snapchat in the world of work. Writing effectively so your business messages shine through today's digital noise is a valuable, sought-after skill for your employability.'
Louise Stansfield, Senior Lecturer, Metropolia Business School, Metropolia University of Applied Sciences, Finland

'I have been managing international initiatives with native and non-native English-speaking colleagues from many countries. This means working together...without ever meeting in person!

English words, especially written words, are the most powerful tool we have in these teams. If they fail, as they sometimes do, no matter what your enthusiasm and talent, the best chance you will ever get is to try again with better English words.

This is why I have used several of Fiona Talbot's books over the years. This latest edition of *How to Write Effective Business English* has some new features that are especially relevant for my work. For instance:

- What to do with paper – printed, even handwritten letters. Paper is here to stay, often in increasingly specialist areas.

- How to manage communication in multinational and virtual teams – including inter-generational teams where leaders are often younger than members.

- How to write when microblogging and instant messaging – and how to write e-mails now that instant messaging and social network sharing make an impact on the style needed.

How to Write Effective Business English makes you aware of the pitfalls you encounter every day you work with written English, and will give you a very good chance to get your message right and powerful today.'
Gianluca Marcellino, Global Retail Industry Manager, Avanade

'*How to Write Effective Business English* is an invaluable toolkit for any business, especially in today's environment of instant, digital, global communication, where the clarity of our language is essential to ensuring that our message is heard as intended. Written in accessible language, covering the many and diverse ways in which we all use written words in our daily working lives, this book really does help create impactful communication.'
Katie Page, Content Director, GlobalData

'An absolute must-read for all business owners and, indeed, businesspeople alike! Perfect for those who want to invigorate their written work to really pack a punch! I never leave my desk without it! Follow Fiona Talbot's wise words and success will follow.'
Paul Corcoran, Chief Executive, Agent Marketing

Third Edition

How to Write Effective Business English

Your guide to excellent professional communication

Fiona Talbot

KoganPage

$26.99

First published in Great Britain and the United States in 2009 by Kogan Page Limited
Second edition published in 2016
Third edition published in 2019

2nd Floor, 45 Gee Street
London
EC1V 3RS
United Kingdom

122 W 27th St, 10th Floor
New York, NY 10001
USA

4737/23 Ansari Road
Daryaganj
New Delhi 110002
India

www.koganpage.com

ISBNs

Hardback   978 1 78966 020 3
Paperback   978 0 7494 9729 3
eBook   978 0 7494 9730 9

British Library Cataloguing-in-Publication Data

A CIP record for this book is available from the British Library.

Library of Congress Cataloging-in-Publication Data
Names: Talbot, Fiona, author.
Title: How to write effective business English : your guide to excellent
    professional communication / Fiona Talbot.
Description: Third edition. | London ; New York : Kogan Page Limited, 2019.
Identifiers: LCCN 2019013425 (print) | LCCN 2019016212 (ebook) | ISBN
    9780749497309 (Ebook) | ISBN 9781789660203 (hardback) | ISBN 9780749497293
    (pbk.)
Subjects: LCSH: English language–Business English–Study and teaching. |
    Business communication–Study and teaching. | English language–Textbooks
    for foreign speakers. | Business writing.
Classification: LCC PE1479.B87 (ebook) | LCC PE1479.B87 T35 2019 (print) |
    DDC 808.06/665–dc23
LC record available at https://lccn.loc.gov/2019013425

Typeset by Integra Software Services, Pondicherry
Print production managed by Jellyfish
Printed and bound by CPI Group (UK) Ltd, Croydon CR0 4YY

With thanks to my clients and readers, my editor Rebecca Bush and all at Kogan Page, for your interest in the wonderful world of #wordpowerskills.

Special thanks go to my dear husband, Colin; to Alexander, Hannah-Maria, Johanna and Daren. It's with great joy that I also see the youngest members of the family, Jude, Dominique and Xanthe, already taking delight in words.

I dedicate this book to you all.

CONTENTS

Introduction 1

01 **Why are you writing?** 3
Who are your readers? 3
What's the purpose of your writing? 4
Readers take just a few seconds to judge your writing 6
How formal or informal do you need to be? 7
Your checklist for action 8

02 **Business writing for today** 9
Winning business through English 9
Academic writing compared to business writing 9
Can you use 'I' in business writing? 10
Listen to readers' feedback 12
Choosing the right style 14
Ideal communication 17
The word power skills system: four easy steps to premier
   business writing 18
Your checklist for action 20

03 **Quality matters** 21
Shine through your writing! 21
To make mistakes is only human 21
How readers can react to written mistakes 22
Further costs of getting your writing wrong 24
You can never fully outsource your writing 27
Checking for mistakes 27
Proofreading tips 28
Your checklist for action 29

04   Writing across generations – for colleagues as well as clients 31

Pool communication strengths: the rewards of
   generational diversity 31

Write to get that job 33

Write to recruit 33

Use word power to develop your career and get the
   results you need 36

Write for your boss 37

When you're the boss, writing brings extra challenges! 39

Your checklist for action 43

05   Telling your story through social media 45

Social media has shaken 'the rules' of business writing 45

Get into the social media mindset 45

Get your business message to anyone, anywhere, anytime 46

What are the key objectives? 48

How do companies shine through their social media
   interaction? 51

Writing that creates trust can create a community 53

The long and the short of it: past, present and future 55

Further writing tips for key channels such as Facebook,
   Twitter and LinkedIn 56

What excites people so much they want to share it? 62

Call people to action – and check it's worked 63

Telling your story 65

Your checklist for action 67

06   Standard or variant English? 69

'Standard' and 'variant' English 69

Writing for both native and non-native English speakers 71

Some surprising problems with English for global
   business 71

Define business English within your company 72

Your checklist for action 73

07 Writing globally? Or in multinational teams? 75
Looking at how you use English at work 75
Converting thoughts into words, then into writing 77
Better to ask if you don't understand something 78
These features can perplex readers too 79
Muddled business writing costs on so many levels 82
Tune in to how English continues to evolve 83
Non-native English writers can have an advantage! 84
Your checklist for action 85

08 E-mail and instant messaging 87
General 87
Writing e-mails 88
E-mail scenarios to watch out for 88
Multilingual and other e-mail threads 89
Structure your e-mails 93
Designing how you write e-mails 94
Instant messaging and texting 97
Your checklist for action 102

09 Punctuation and grammar tips 105
Why punctuation and grammar matter 105
Punctuation and other marks 106
Parts of speech and other grammar 107
Paragraphs 112
Verbs and tenses 113
Agreement of subject and verb 115
Comparison 118
Fluidity in writing 119
Your checklist for action 120

10   Practical conventions and common confusions 121

Writing a date 121

Time 124

Numbers 126

Measurements 127

Words that can confuse both native English and non-native
    English writers 128

Acronyms 130

Active and passive 132

Nominalization 133

Your checklist for action 134

11   Paper is here to stay 135

Letters 137

Traditional letter format 138

When flexibility is key, you need to adapt letter-writing
    templates 140

A letter that involves the reader with the company's
    narrative 142

Specific tips about addressing letters 144

CVs/résumés and cover letters 144

Your checklist for action 147

**Conclusion: what will you do
differently – and better?** 149

Introduction

Don't just be enthusiastic in #socialmedia. It's passion that engages readers throughout all your corporate communications.

FIONA TALBOT

Who is this book for? Think about sector, culture and generation

If you're in business (or are preparing to enter the workplace) you'll see how the written word dominates in business communication today, largely due to the unremitting rise in e-writing. Everyone now has a voice and almost everyone is now a writer, though few are actually trained in this.

That's why this business English primer is ideal for both native and non-native English speakers (proficient at intermediate level and above). Its extensive task-based guidance helps you develop the highly prized workplace skills that bosses cry out for.

Increasingly, English is the language of choice in the information age, widely used on the web and in multinational gatherings. Staggeringly, it's estimated that English is spoken by a quarter of the world's population (and rising), as a language of common global currency. So it becomes a powerful tool for communication and inclusion – as long as you realize that you'll need to tailor it to suit the expectations of:

- your target business sector;
- your target culture and the variety of English they use;
- today's multigenerational workplace and client base.

Ensure content of value in everything you write

Effective writing today isn't just about reports, presentations, letters and so on. Writing skills arguably matter more than ever in e-mail, instant messaging, the plain English needed for technical documents and coding, marketing, PR, infographics and social media – even in video storytelling and audiobooks where scripts are also key.

Today's need is for content of value and I'm keen that you develop a passion for business writing that creates a consistently good reader experience. My word power skills writing system will help you do that. And don't let's forget, content means every word you use in every business writing task you do.

Everything should add up to make great corporate communication.

Bosses need people who can write well, grab attention for the right reasons, influence, persuade, reflect brand and values, and enhance reputation... preferably in the shortest time. That's why the book describes scenarios every office encounters – and the real-life examples make great discussion points with bosses and colleagues alike. You'll be able to customize the tips for every writing task.

Enjoy getting results!

I hope you enjoy this guide to excellent professional communication, which should also aid your employability and future career prospects.

Enjoy using the concept of word power skills (which I tag #wordpowerskills in social media posts) as a free yet highly valued resource – indeed my clients find they buzz with it!

Good luck on your journey to success!

Fiona Talbot
TQI Word Power Skills
www.wordpowerskills.com

01
Why are you writing?

Who are your readers?

You'll see that I use the terms readers, target readership, customers and audience interchangeably. A 'customer' can be a person who buys goods or services from a business, or can be a person you deal with in the course of your daily work. The term applies just as much to internal colleagues, suppliers, those in the public sector, etc as it does to those who are external consumers.

Your audience can be anyone and everyone

Where you know your target audience's profile, you have an immediate advantage. Today's business is all about customizing products and services to suit the individual customer. It works for communication too. By what means does your target readership like to receive messages? Are you able to match their needs, generational and cultural expectations, and engage their interest because you know their profile? It's great news if you can.

The potential global reach of your e-writing (which includes social media) is particularly exciting. The start-up business (maybe even operating from home) can have as loud a voice as the large corporate. Your messages may (perhaps unexpectedly) be forwarded on by others, even go viral. So every business message, personalized or not, had better be professional! Nothing should be open to misinterpretation or cause offence, even unintentionally.

Many practical examples and scenarios in this book relate to sales or customer pitches. Because we're all consumers in our private lives, we can relate to and understand these examples. The concepts apply equally to every scenario in the list that follows. Think of lobbying; think of politics; think of charities; think of fundraising; think of promotions; think of the clarity needed for writing clear instructions in coding (one of the fastest-growing career paths in the 21st century); think of the increasing pressure on the medical and legal professions (as just two examples) to write in plain, reader-centred English.

What's the purpose of your writing?

People sometimes think of business writing as a 'soft' skill as opposed to the 'hard' skills of finance, law, IT, etc. But I think this description is misleading. The label 'soft' can give the impression that business writing is an easy skill, and it isn't. Business writing has a critical impact on the whole business cycle; it can win business, it can lose business and it can communicate the framework by which results can be achieved.

So, at the outset of my training workshops, I always take time to ask people why they actually write in their job and what outcomes they seek, individually and as teams. Unless they are marketers by profession, the following aspects of business writing usually come top of the list:

1 to inform or record;

2 to cascade information;

3 for compliance;

4 to seek information;

5 to write specifications;

6 to achieve a standard;

7 to write reports with recommendations;

8 to persuade;

9 to promote services.

Usually far lower on the list (and sometimes only when prompted by me, on the lines of 'Aren't there any other reasons?'), they say:

- to engage interest and involve;
- to get the right results;
- to sell;
- to support customers;
- to improve life for customers;
- to create a following;
- to influence;
- to change things/innovate/disrupt;
- to enhance brand and reputation;
- to show our personality;
- to reflect our values;
- to eat, breathe and live our vision.

Notice how the most inspirational aspects of writing are the ones that are listed as an afterthought!

Why is this? Maybe companies need to focus more on how powerful business writing can be and how *all* employees need to think creatively about how best to harness this virtually free resource. Think about what writing really means for your company.

Activity: Each time you write, first ask yourself:

- Why am I writing?
- What are my/my company's values and objectives?
- Do I have a definite or outline profile for my target audience?
- What are their values and needs?
- How will I align my message(s)?
- What style, vocabulary (and medium, where you have a choice) are likely to suit them best?
- How can I project my company's 'personality' and create an opportunity to shine myself?

Your writing won't work if you don't first plan what you need to achieve!

Readers take just a few seconds to judge your writing

The written word is unforgiving. When I read, I judge what I see written for what it is. If I'm seeking products or services, what I see can be what I think I get. If it is your writing, I'll judge both you as an individual and your company on the basis of how you expressed yourself at that point in time. That's how important writing is.

It's commercial folly that many written messages lead to confusion and misunderstanding – even when a company is writing in its native language. Poor writing can also lead to customer complaints. And the worst scenarios are where customers walk away from the companies concerned, and tell others about the bad experience they have received or think they have received. That's the impact that ineffective writing can have. It becomes quite clear that if, as customers, we don't understand or like what supplier A is writing, we prefer to buy from supplier B, who cares enough about our needs to get the message right. And if this takes less time, so much the better.

No body language signals in writing

When we communicate face to face, people around us attach importance to the signals given by our body language. These are said to account for 55 per cent of the impact we make when giving a talk. Our voice can account for perhaps 38 per cent – and our words just 7 per cent.

This is because, in face-to-face communication, unlike writing, we don't need to focus just on words. We can ask if we aren't sure what is being said. We can look for clues from the speaker's facial expression or tone as to the gravity or levity of the subject matter. These will help our understanding and focus our attention (or not!).

But with writing now taking centre stage in today's workplace (think e-mail, instant messaging, social media), words are actually *crucial*. Unless the writer is there in front of you, time will elapse before you get answers to any questions you have. That is, if you have the time or inclination to ask questions! At the very least, it means that writers need to think twice, spellcheck – in fact, double-check – that their words are saying what they mean them to say.

How formal or informal do you need to be?

Business writing is in a state of flux and is increasingly diverse in style. Different styles often coexist within the same company. It can be bewildering for reader and writer alike as I'll show throughout the book. Generally speaking, the move is towards more 'people' words and more informality.

This can be a special challenge for some cultures. Asian cultures, for example, place great emphasis on hierarchy, where people of senior grades are treated with noticeably more deference and respect than those in junior grades. Informality can also be a challenge for nationalities where there is a distinction between a familiar and a formal form of the pronoun 'you'. Even Western cultures can do this; for example, French makes a distinction between *tu* (informal) and *vous* (formal). Such cultures can try to compensate for this lack of distinction by writing more elaborately for what they see as the 'formal you' as opposed to the 'informal you'. This doesn't necessarily work.

Your checklist for action

- Recognize writing as a fundamental career skill for you as an individual and for your business.
- Develop and improve your writing at every opportunity to impress, influence, and boost your employability.
- Remember that English business writing – in its many forms – is your most common route to market. Be the best.

02
Business writing for today

Winning business through English

Years ago, it often took longer to do deals than it does today. The ritual involved initial telephone enquiries or formal letters of introduction, and preliminary and follow-up meetings for two or more parties to 'sound each other out'.

Today the layer of detailed introductions and small talk has partly given way to addressing the real purpose: to drive business success. Upcoming generations increasingly ditch phone calls and meetings where they can, preferring the written word to achieve results.

But there may be a gap between how you were taught to write English at school or university and how you need to write it for business.

Academic writing compared to business writing

These are two almost entirely different genres. Their goals are different, and they require different approaches.

Academic writing requirements

Students are generally required to write structured essays, research papers and theses. These are largely marked on the basis of how well students have managed to access the right information, process this, show prose/composition skills and accuracy, and conform to a fairly standard presentation format. By and large, the structure involves a beginning (topic and purpose), a middle (evidence and argument, or thesis) and an end (conclusion). The words and tone used must be relevant for the world of academe. This can require a formal, objective, impersonal style and an extensive, specialized vocabulary can gain marks.

Business writing requirements

The workplace is quite different. Yes, you certainly need to know how to access the right information and process this when you write. You need to be accurate too. Many companies require you to follow a standard house style. But, increasingly, you may be encouraged to make suggestions about how the house style could evolve, in view of business circumstances and customers' needs – and changing communication expectations. This is great news for upcoming generations who can make their mark more quickly than ever before!

Attention spans are lessening, thanks to the 'I-want-it-now' immediacy of the information age. There are fewer occasions when business writing is seen to have the academic-style beginning, middle and end structure (other than in certain formal reports). Seize the opportunity to develop communication skills that you may not have come across previously.

Can you use 'I' in business writing?

Assess which elements of school writing to discard when you enter the workplace. For example, time after time I hear 'We were taught at school that we can't use "I" and "we" in the same sentence in a letter', or 'You can't write "I" in business; it must always be "we"'.

Many companies feel that a key driver of business success is empowerment of the individual. For them, it's about everyone being given the power and encouragement to make a difference within their organization. There may be 'no I in team' (I'm using this management speak ironically here!) but to embrace the concept of 'I/me' can be crucial. And such companies may also encourage you to write 'we' (even within the same piece of writing), to demonstrate that each person is an integral part of the total company.

You will certainly find plenty of evidence from companies worldwide that you can use 'I' and 'we' within your sentences – but always research company culture first.

Other things you may wish to 'unlearn'

You may have been taught that you cannot begin a sentence with 'And' or 'But'. Actually, you can – and many acclaimed writers do. For traditionalists, let me mention the famous English novelist Jane Austen as one example. I often begin sentences this way throughout the book, as the style seems relevant for today. This is largely because e-writing is today's predominant business writing and its style is mostly halfway between conversation and formal writing. Some call it 'talk writing'. There's a knock-on effect on the way people write other business documentation. It's not about 'dumbing down'; it's about expressing facts simply, in accessible writing that speaks to people.

It's true to say that if I had a specific customer or line manager who hated sentences beginning with 'And' or 'But', I wouldn't use that style with them. Similarly, if my publishers didn't accept the style, I would avoid it – but they agree it's appropriate for standard business English writing. Naturally, it is essential to be reader-driven when you write. As I cannot have the advantage of knowing each of you, my readers, I will use a generic style.

But where you can, put out your antennae and tune in to what people don't like! There are always alternatives you can choose.

Here are some examples that regularly crop up in my training workshops. Where at all possible, people prefer to read:

- 'For this to work, you/we need to...' rather than 'It must be done.'

- 'Thank you for bringing this to our attention' rather than 'We note...'

- 'So that we can reach our targets, please could I have these figures tomorrow?' rather than 'I need these figures tomorrow.'

- 'We are really sorry we can't help (because...)' rather than 'We can't help.'

See the pattern emerging? People tend not to like terseness and they like to be given reasons why things have to be done. Ask for assistance, and they are more likely to help!

It can help to draw up two lists. One can be a list of 'Things to avoid' and includes any expressions or style that you know your boss doesn't like or that your readers have criticized. On the plus side, then draw up a list of 'Things that worked' and get into the habit of using these.

Listen to readers' feedback

Ask readers for feedback on your business English writing. You'll learn so much. Companies who take the time to do so find that readers routinely comment that:

- they feel patronized by poorly written letters;

- they can feel insulted by writers' lack of attention to the right detail;

- they don't sense the 'human touch' in much of the language used in business writing;

- they can feel so angered by correspondence that, where they can do so, they'll walk away from the business concerned;

- they dislike unnecessary jargon (words or expressions used by a particular profession or group that may be difficult for others to understand), over-complicated sentences and confusing use of words;

- they are offended when their personal details are incorrect.

Do re-read this list from time to time. Never lose sight of how readers may react. I'll deal with all these aspects of writing in this book but will just highlight one of the most common now. It's this: what do you think the lack of the 'human touch' in writing could mean? Is it the fact that business writers actively avoid using 'people' words such as 'you' and 'we'? Let me demonstrate. A company writes to a client on the following lines:

Dear Sir

Re: Policy XYZ

It has come to the company's attention that the aforementioned policy that is about to expire has not yet been renewed. I enclose a renewal form, which you need to return within seven days, otherwise you will no longer be afforded cover.

Yours faithfully

John Smith

Smith and Co

Some companies still use this stilted, old-fashioned English and I cannot imagine why. Especially now, as we live in a world where customers increasingly expect to feel the personal touch – and to feel valued. So let's redesign the message, using people words and more modern English.

Dear (client's name)

Invitation to renew your policy

We would like to invite you to renew your policy, which expires shortly (date) and would like to ensure that you continue to have the cover you need.

So please could you read, then complete as necessary, the enclosed renewal form, and return it to us by (date)?

If you have any questions, I'm here to help (telephone number and/or e-mail address).

With thanks

Yours sincerely

John Smith

Smith and Co

A letter from my car insurers impressed me easily by ending with a human touch:

Thank you

Thank you again for insuring your car with us for another year and we wish you a safe year of driving.

Try to be personable through your writing. People do like it.

Choosing the right style

More examples follow, showing how writers and readers alike can be confused by differing styles of written English within their own company.

1 Therefore, although obviously we cannot make any assessment about the matter in hand on this occasion, we will nevertheless take cognizance of the contents of your letter and will forthwith forward a copy thereof to the managing director who has the appropriate responsibility for investigating any issues raised.

2 Done.

3 Thanks loads.

The style in the first example is extremely formal English and quite old-fashioned. You can see what I term barrier words: 'therefore', 'obviously', 'nevertheless' and 'forthwith'. They are all correct English, but they can make readers feel distanced. The majority of readers will probably view the writer as condescending towards an 'inferior' reader, rather than communicating with a valued customer.

The one word 'Done' in the second example is a common e-mail response these days, when someone has asked a question such as 'Have you completed this action?' Those who write the one-word reply usually feel they are very effective workers and communicators. What they don't see is the irritated face on the receiving end of the e-mail! The one-word reply is so often seen as plain rude. Just by adding four words and changing the reply to 'Yes, I have done that' you can make the writing seem less curt and more polite. As people comment on this in so many training workshops that I run, it's well worth a mention here.

The third example is very informal and we see it a lot in business today. It's very friendly but it's best to be aware that some readers may still consider it unprofessional and inappropriate for corporate communication. Some writers say they are only that informal when writing for someone they really know. That's fine. But also be aware there can be a problem when e-mails may continue in threads – and be forwarded unexpectedly to external recipients too. I've seen time and time again where unguarded colloquial language has caused unintended embarrassment.

CASE STUDY   Choosing the right style

One major supermarket chain issued a product recall. They had discovered that an axe they sold had a design fault. The head could become detached from the handle.

The retailer decided to ditch the old-fashioned approach to a product recall notice, which in the past might have started:

> A decision has been taken to recall (description of product) as it has been found to be faulty. Please return the product immediately for a refund... (full details of method...).

Instead, they decided to refresh their style and the product recall notice included these words:

> Our (product details) axe would be fantastic apart from the fact that the head can become detached from the handle. Quite clearly, this is not on so we have decided that you need to know. Thankfully no one has been hurt. (They then go on to detail how customers can get a refund).

The recall ends with 'It goes without saying... we're very sorry indeed.'

What do you think of this approach? At first sight, many people quite like it. When they read on, they often change their mind, finding the style too light-hearted for a potentially highly dangerous scenario. And how does the retailer know that nobody has been hurt, just because they hadn't been notified before they posted the recall?

Effective business writing has to 'think ahead' for all sorts of possibilities – and adopt the right style for the situation as well as the audience.

You are likely to see contrasts in business English writing in your company. Consider whether taking a middle course, a median between an overly formal or overly informal style, might work best, to avoid unnecessarily confusing styles.

Ideal communication

It's hard to define ideal business communication but this summary is useful:

> Effective written communication is when the correct, concise, current message is sent out to the primary receiver(s), then onwards without distortion to further receivers to generate the required response.

Let me amplify. Sometimes we write to someone simply to inform them of something. They then remain the primary receiver. The only response we require is one that favours the way we have delivered the message (both on a personal and a company level). Probably more often our aim when we write is to do more than simply inform. We're looking for the receiver(s) to like our style and *to do* something too. Our writing should influence them and actively enable this. It's crucial that it is understood by all who read it (first-hand or forwarded on), so we achieve our objectives and cover everyone's needs.

Why include the word 'current' in the formula? This is because so often people systematically address the first two points I list, but then forget to update the information. Then the best-laid plans get messed up.

Here's an example. An external trainer is going to deliver a course for 10 members of a company's staff. One week earlier, their manager issues joining instructions to all attending. The course is to be held in the Byfield Room in a hotel the company uses. The trainer has been e-mailed the full list of names and has asked the company to notify any changes before the day.

By the day of the training no changes have been communicated and the trainer arrives for set-up. He finds that the hotel has changed the venue to the Smithson Room. This hasn't been laid out as requested and there's no overhead projector, which is crucial. By the time the course is due to start at 9 am, only seven attendees have turned up. The trainer texts then calls the company to check

but the relevant manager isn't available. So the trainer puts back the start time, in case the missing delegates are held up in traffic.

He later finds out that the company knew that three delegates would be unable to attend on the day.

Can you see why the failure to relay changes cost money and affected performance? Both the hotel and the client company were at fault here. Although the course went ahead, there was unnecessary hassle and a distinct lack of professionalism. It also made for a chaotic scene, which was likely to undermine delegates' perception of the whole day. This kind of thing happens all too frequently. It comes as a direct result of people not reading and responding and messaging to update and inform others of changing or changed circumstances. A minor series of events and failure to update communication can turn a well-organized programme into an unprofessional shambles.

The word power skills system: four easy steps to premier business writing

The system uses the idea of 'a ladder of success', in which you start at the bottom (Step 1) and systematically climb to success (beyond Step 4) as follows:

Step 1

Be correct:

- Know what your writing needs to achieve, alongside what your company needs to achieve.
- Reflect your company's values and personality, and project 'brand you'.
- At the very least, match readers' minimum expectations.
- Ensure that your writing is free of mistakes.

Your business communication will fail if you get your basics wrong.

Step 2

Be clear:

- Use plain English and express facts as simply as possible.
- Edit so that your main points are easily understood.
- Use headings and sub-headings to highlight key information.

Confused messages undermine your objectives. They can lose you custom too.

Step 3

Make the right impact:

- Use the right words to grab attention, and a layout that gets noticed for the right reasons.
- Paint a picture with your words and use verbs to convey action and ownership of who does what and when.
- Use the right style to present yourself and your company well.
- Create opportunities.

The right impact differentiates you from competitors and helps bring about the responses you need. There's more about this in Chapter 5 on social media.

Step 4

Focus on readers as your customers:

- Get to know as much about them as you can, so you can write from their perspective.
- Empathize with them and make your content interesting, so that they want to read.
- Favour positive, proactive words to engage, persuade, influence – and create a dialogue and following, where needed.

- Avoid words that put up barriers, and avoid unnecessary jargon.
- Instead choose words that convey a virtual handshake, to pull people towards you.

Use your written words to satisfy and, if possible, delight your customers.

Your checklist for action

- Realize that your readers and customers are likely to have a negative impression of or even reject ineffective writing.
- Evaluate feedback on your writing. You can do this simply by checking your answers to questions such as the following:
  - When you send an e-mail or other message, do people often not bother to read it?
  - Do you have to send out the same message more than once to get the reply you need?
  - Do people ever congratulate you or complain about the tone of your message?
  - Are your letters, reports, e-mails or other messages significantly longer than those of your colleagues? If so, why is that?
  - When you receive new details, do you always update people who need to know?
- Understand the differences between academic writing and business English writing.
- Remember business writing is results-focused and tending to become more informal, adopting much of the style of e-writing where material is presented in bite-sized chunks.
- Be prepared to unlearn some of the rules you may have learnt at school – or now think up some useful ones you weren't taught!

03
Quality matters

Shine through your writing!

How do you want to be seen? What do you want to be remembered for? To be professional, it's best to get your business English writing right, first time and every time. Contribute to your own success by understanding that each bit of business writing you send out can be (indeed, should be) viewed as an advertisement for 'brand you' as well as for your company. Written words are 'frozen' in the point of time in which they were written: judged for what they are, when we're not there to explain them.

To succeed they have to be the right words for your commercial purpose, or you'll fall at the first hurdle. They also have to be right from your readers' point of view, or you'll fall at the second hurdle. And what a missed opportunity if you don't write to impress: to be the best you can. Don't settle for less; the competition won't!

To make mistakes is only human

The trouble is that whatever our proficiency in a language, we're all likely to make written mistakes sometimes. A tip that really works is: don't expect your writing to be right! You often achieve better results by expecting it to be wrong. That way you are more likely to:

- spot mistakes at draft stage;
- remove them before sending writing out;
- present a totally professional corporate image.

Checking, even double-checking your writing before you send may take more time but pays great dividends. That's why many companies ask me to train staff to do exactly this, because although it may be second nature to you, that's not the case for many.

How readers can react to written mistakes

Just take a look at two problematic sentences and let's see how readers might react.

1 Thank you for your order. You are demanded to send payment within 30 days.

First of all, the expression 'you are demanded' isn't correct English. It's better to write something on the lines of 'Please send payment within 30 days' or 'You are requested to pay within 30 days.' In English there is an expression 'to demand payment' but it has a very strong connotation. It's generally used for the final notice before a company pursues legal action, to collect money owing to it in an overdue account. When the expression is used validly, it would be on the following lines: 'This is a final demand for payment (within 30 days) of your outstanding account.'

So in our first example we have an outright grammatical mistake. But the wrong tone can also count as a writing mistake.

Let's look at the text again: 'Thank you for your order. You are demanded to send payment within 30 days.' Although the reader sees the initial words 'Thank you', the next sentence introduces a harsh, accusatory tone. Yet this is clearly one of the first points of contact between customer and company. The order has just been placed: 'Thank you for your order' tells us that. So is the customer going to feel that this is a nice company to do business with? I don't think so.

In business, when new customers place their orders, we should make this a very positive experience for them. If a company can't be bothered to write well here, then the indicators are not good for future business success. Customers usually have a choice: there is likely to be an alternative company that they like to do business with. Which would you choose?

2 We can certainly provide the services you request in principal.

Homonyms are words that have the same or similar sound and sometimes the same spelling as another but whose meanings are different (more on this in Chapter 10). But let's just take a look here at two words that are frequently confused by native English and non-native English writers alike. They are:

Principal: an adjective generally meaning first in importance; also a noun meaning a chief or senior person, or an original sum of money for investment.

Principle: a noun meaning a fundamental truth or quality; a rule or belief governing a person's morally correct behaviour and attitudes.

In the second example, unfortunately the writer has chosen the wrong version of the homonym. The correct word would be 'principle'. Some readers may not mind this; some will not notice. But some will make a value judgement: this is wrong!

It may be unfair but just one wrong word can undermine readers' perception of a writer's or a company's professionalism. It can also distract readers' attention away from the writer's key message.

Although I've just highlighted some mistakes, I'm not suggesting a 'red pen' approach. Some managers use a red pen to highlight an employee's written mistakes, in a clearly unsupportive way. This approach is particularly unfair to dyslexic employees and can really demotivate staff generally. Helpful suggestions work much better.

It's true that sometimes you just have to write the way your line manager suggests. But it's always better to know the reasons why they consider one way better than another. Even in UK English you can write certain words in two ways, both of which are correct. You can write 'recognize' or 'recognise', or 'judgement' or 'judgment' – and it can be personal or company preference that dictates which you use. If you don't understand the reasons why you must write a certain way, your manager owes it to you to explain why. But you also owe it to yourself to ask why.

It's in your own interest to know if you make mistakes. Readers may comment on them. In business you can't afford to 'bury your head in the sand' – in other words, just because you don't acknowledge something, that does not mean it does not exist! Problems do occur and every business needs to identify them. How else can we seek solutions and get things right?

Making mistakes may be human, but we do need to focus on quality and it's best to define what we mean by this. Does it mean 'top quality' or simply 'acceptable'? You might be surprised at the number of businesses who don't define what they expect the quality of their written output to be – not just from their point of view but from their customers' perspective. This lines up with one aspect of Step 1 on the ladder of success, described in Chapter 2.

Further costs of getting your writing wrong

We saw how things can go wrong when we don't update written messages in the light of changed circumstances. The following scenario also shows other costs businesses can pay for getting writing wrong.

I submitted a database entry on my business to a company for inclusion in a Europe-wide guide. Their fee seemed reasonable, given the likely exposure to new business. I had to follow their format with limited word count, so my entry was as follows:

TQI Word Power Skills training

Activity: A UK company that provides business support services for every type of business. It provides business English services to help with marketing literature and communication skills training.

Services include editing, text correction or fine tuning, quality assurance, proof-reading, group workshops, individual coaching in business English and cross-cultural briefing.

These innovative, fully confidential business services are designed to help you assure the quality of your service or product and help you hit your commercial target first and every time.

TQI Word Power Skills training offers businesses of all types and sizes expert and affordable solutions for their business English needs, together with international experience from previous consultancy in the Netherlands.

Co-operation request: TQI Word Power Skills Training seeks companies requiring these services.

A few weeks later I received an invoice from the company concerned. Attached to this was a copy of the entry as it had actually appeared. Unknown to me, the copy had already gone live, Europewide, one month before I received the invoice. The entry was now the one shown below. It includes a number of errors, made when the company inputted my original wording onto the database. Can you spot these mistakes?

TQI Word Power Skills training

Activity: UK company that provides business support services for every type of business, it provides Business english services to help with marketing literature and communication skills training.

Services include editing, text correction or fine tuning, quality assurance, proof reading, group workshops, infividual coaching in Business English and inter cultural breifing.

These Innovative fully confidential business services are designed to help you assure the quality of your service or product and help you hit your commercial target first and every time.

TQI Word Power Skills training offers businesses of all types and sizes expert and affordable solutions for their business English needs, international expereince from previous consultancy in the Netherland.

Co-operation request: TQI Word Power Skills Training seeks companies that require there servces.

Quite understandably, I was not at all happy, especially when presented with an invoice to pay for this appalling entry. Can you see why? Look closely and you'll see at least one mistake in each paragraph. Some are spelling mistakes, such as 'infivdual' for 'individual', 'breifing' for 'briefing' and 'expereince' for 'experience'. Some are inconsistencies, such as business English and Business English. Both may be used, but it's better style to keep to a single use, certainly within one paragraph. The word innovative suddenly has a capital 'I', thus we find 'Innovative' even though the word is mid-sentence. And the list goes on. One thing is sure: nobody ran a spellcheck or grammar check.

What ultimately was the cost of this regrettable incident? Well, it might surprise you that there was an actual cost to pay on as many as five different levels! You see:

1 I refused to pay the invoice because the entry was incorrect, so the company suffered the loss of that income.

2 That company then had to redraft a correct entry, which cost them duplication of work.

3 They then had to make arrangements to replace the incorrect entry at another time, at their own further cost.

4 One cost to my company was in terms of seriously undermined professional credibility (both in the short and long term).

5 I also paid a price in losing the publicity time-slot I had requested. A later entry was not ideal for my business purpose.

Can you see how such an apparently low-key set of mistakes can have a disastrous effect on the professional credibility of a company that's operating internationally?

In the final analysis, although the mistakes were not mine, they appeared to be mine. It was my company name and my details that appeared... which leads me to the next section.

You can never fully outsource your writing

What that last episode taught me was this: not to assume that because the version I sent for publishing was correct, the published version would be correct too. The advertising company used Apple Macs and did not just cut and paste my Word document: they retyped the copy themselves. Whether or not this was the case, I should have asked to see the final proof before publication. Printers often provide this as a matter of course, to cover themselves against complaints at a later stage. But note that word 'often' – it's not the same as 'always'!

If you outsource something and it goes wrong, the backlash becomes yours too. You can't outsource responsibility!

Checking for mistakes

Let me reinforce the message: expect mistakes in your writing draft. Here's an analogy. When I was learning to drive, my teacher gave me invaluable advice. I was told to imagine everyone on the road was a maniac. That way, he explained, I would never be complacent but always alert to the fact that mistakes inevitably happen. And I'd be a better driver as a result, more likely to respond quickly to ever-changing situations and take corrective action. Can you see how easily the advice applies to checking for mistakes in your English writing too?

Proofreading tips

Check everything you write before you send it out. Here are tips to help:

- Allow sufficient time for your proofreading. If you rush, you may still overlook the mistakes you are looking for.

- It can be easier to proofread on paper than on a computer screen (though be eco-friendly about this).

- Use a standard or online dictionary or grammar book to help you, or your computer's spelling and grammar check (set on the correct variant of English for your target audience). Remember this is not fail-safe. It may let the wrong word(s) through, especially homonyms, for example 'brake' for 'break', 'there' for 'their' and so on.

- Watch out for autocorrect wrongly changing your correct words such as 'its' to 'it's' or 'definitely' to 'defiantly'.

- Try reading your lines backwards (people sometimes use a ruler to read one line at a time, to avoid distraction). You don't check meaning this way, but you can check the words are written correctly.

- Now check for meaning and logic.

- Make a self-help list of any words you regularly get wrong, so that you can check them quickly and effectively next time you write them.

Your checklist for action

- Understand that mistakes can and do happen.

- Make sure you take steps to minimize this, such as running spellcheck and grammar check in the right variety of English.

- Realize mistakes aren't just about spelling and grammar. They can also be when words are left out, when sentences confuse, or facts are presented in a disorderly way that might even distort the correct message.

- Understand the longer-term impact mistakes may have (and how these can in turn impact on you and your company). Highlight this to others.

- Do an overall check of your writing before you issue it.

- If you are not sure of something, ask for help from someone who will know.

04
Writing across generations – for colleagues as well as clients

Pool communication strengths: the rewards of generational diversity

Effective writing is increasingly the route to getting into an organization. You need the foundations in place. Once in, if you are to develop your career, you'll need to fine-tune your communication skills – not just to the task but also to the differing levels of readership you'll encounter.

In later chapters, I'll show you how to write across cultures in an international context. Right now, I'd like to touch on how to write across generations.

There can be up to five generations in today's workplace and client base, commonly classified as:

- The Silent Generation/Traditionalists – born before 1946
- Baby Boomers – born between 1946 and 1964
- Generation X – born between 1965 and 1980

- Generation Y, or Millennials – born between 1981 and 1997
- Generation Z, or Post-Millennials – born after 1997

This mix brings different communication perspectives – and successful organizations know how to create a winning fusion of their styles. Interestingly, millennials and post-millennials – who I prefer to call 'upcoming generations' – are estimated to become 75 per cent of the workforce by 2030. They come into the workplace knowing they have a voice and, understandably, they expect it to be heard.

So what advice can I give all generations about how to write effectively in business today? Well, in terms of business writing, until fairly recently, new entrants to the workplace were expected to mirror the writing style of their seniors. Young graduates would write to clients 'We await your instructions at your earliest convenience' and the like. Though it wasn't their natural language, they complied with convention and deferred to their managers.

How times have changed! Of course, every person is different, but the broad trends show that upcoming generations are unlikely to be attracted in the first place to an organization that doesn't use the accessible language they're familiar with. They also prefer to work for someone they trust, which they'll glean via the values they see communicated.

They noticeably communicate all the time, not so much by phone calls or meetings but yes, by written words – in instant messaging or e-mails. Being kept in the loop comes naturally to them and is a key skill that their bosses from previous generations desire, but don't always manage.

In turn, upcoming generations must learn how to write successfully with preceding ones at work, as well as for multigenerational client bases, to secure buy-in to messages and persuade – especially where the preceding generations hold greater influence, experience and purchasing power. The majority of communication around us today is actually noise. Older managers can complain that younger generations don't always get to the point. The latter can complain that organizations aren't consistently communicating the values they say they're committed to.

I'd say business writing is ineffective and actually unhelpful if it doesn't lead to action, reaction or results. Now more than ever, generations need to work together in the challenging balancing act of getting writing to work. The rewards of sharing perspectives positively via generational diversity are high.

So here are some suggested steps to help, set out to match the stages in a typical career path.

Write to get that job

This is the first step in your career cycle. Research and get a feel for the brand of the organization you're applying to. Then use the #wordpowerskills writing system I've shown you earlier in the book, to help you promote 'brand you'. There's also more help on CVs/résumés later on. But here, let's focus on: What can you best deliver? What will you be passionate about in the job you seek? Why that organization?

In any written interaction with a prospective employer, cover these aspects. Don't then overlook the equally important bits such as:

- matching your answers to all the questions asked;
- vetting for mistakes;
- caring about presentation.

Write to recruit

Attraction and retention

Growing organizations hire. Once in, you may have to help to recruit others to join too.

Upcoming generations don't generally expect a job for life anymore. They see economic uncertainties all around them, so they seek something that interests them and expect to develop skills to enable them to move on. It does cause companies costly high staff turnover as a result – so increasingly, business writing plays an essential role, both to attract and retain.

Whether you use an agency or write job ads in-house, everything needs to align with your actual workplace communication and values.

Also, alongside professional networks such as LinkedIn, your tech-savvy, potential new-entrant employees will be looking for work via Twitter, Facebook and other channels. They are likely to be showcasing their talents on Instagram, YouTube and Snapchat and ever-emerging platforms. If you check these out you'll get a feel for what it would be like to work with them. In turn, they will be checking out how (or if) you showcase your business – and making judgements whether *they* are interested in *you*.

Communicate your values – show how you give something back

You need to stay credible in everything you write. Even if you hire a recruitment company, your organization is ultimately responsible for all wording used. Get it wrong and all generations will see through you.

Let's look at what today's workplace entrants generally expect:

- Openness, fairness and social responsibility.
- Authenticity.
- A good and caring workplace experience.
- Development on the job.

Is there anything else you would add to this list? What can your organization offer?

CASE STUDY   Communicating complex ideas simply

Let's look at wording used at Nationwide, the world's largest mutual financial institution. In the past we would have expected traditional writing there. But if we analyse their current language we find an inclusive strapline: 'Everyday people, helping everyday people.' This inclusivity concept is consolidated in articles on their website that contain a strong community slant.

In very simple terms they manage to communicate complex ideas: the mark of really effective business writing. Their mission and values are summed up as PRIDE (in itself an acronym that cleverly implies diversity), as follows:

What are our Pride values?

Putting our members and their money first

Rising to the challenge

Inspiring trust

Doing the right thing in the right way

Excelling at relationships

It's valuable to tune in to how companies are successfully adapting yesterday's language to today's needs. You'll find it a real eye-opener.

Writing must underpin the candidate experience

It's staggering how many organizations can get this so wrong – and the generations who know how to use their voice will quickly share this with others. Posting a great ad is only part of the candidate experience that you will be judged on. Effective writing is courteous and it's really expected throughout the recruitment process. It acknowledges applicants' submissions, keeps them in the loop as to how their application is doing, with all time frames set out and adhered to. And don't forget, upcoming generations won't be expecting (or even wait?) to hear from you in three weeks' time when three hours can seem ages to them! Ditch the procrastination: speedy e-mails or instant messaging fit the bill here.

Effective writing also congratulates them if they succeed, and definitely thanks them for their interest even if they don't. Sounds obvious? I'm pleased you think so. Just make sure your organization complies. It really can set you apart for all the right reasons.

Use word power to develop your career and get the results you need

Mid-career and onwards is a time to ensure your business writing doesn't lose its vitality to sell your messages, whatever your business is. Keep up the momentum to propel your career forward.

Step 3 in the writing system I show in Chapter 2 comes into its own right now. Carefully chosen and powerful words don't just sell products or services: they also sell the personalities behind them. In turn they enable the desired responses from colleagues and client base alike.

To give you an idea of powerful words that engage, energize and persuade, in the box on the opposite page is a list of words that delegates at my workshops consistently cite, with relish.

What words do you see as valuable power words in your chosen career path? If you're not currently using them, then why aren't you? Start now! Effective writing mid-career can very much be about getting the right mix of blending in and making your mark, to get noticed for the right reasons.

A word of caution: only use power words validly. A finance director in a major retail company who wrote an e-mail to his team exclaiming 'work is fun!' found the reaction much less positive than he expected. Such words may be right for employees in Silicon Valley – but they just didn't feel right for his audience. Another director who e-mailed: 'I'm fired up about this project! Let's work together to get it going' got the team fully involved. Those words, and that inclusivity, worked for them.

List of power words

you   results   health   guarantee   love   discover

proven   safe   low-cost   save   new   we

value for money   pioneering   cost-effective   advice

help   support   now   immediate   fast   today   easy

effective   benefits   advantages   integrity   reputation

quality   expert   expertise   breakthrough   world-class

disruptive   innovative   valuable   professional   best

premier   excellence   authentic   eco-friendly   unrivalled

passionate   inspirational   please   thank you   talented

amazing   awesome   exciting   friendly   personable

reliable   up-to-date   caring   responsible   collaborative

trust   well-informed   sharing

Write for your boss

I mention the need to blend in, because you do need to check out how bosses expect you to write. Look at their writing. Is there a generational style; a corporate house style? Beyond that, do people write differently for each target audience? Tune in.

Analyse why you've been hired. Was it because you are tech-savvy and/or you're buzzing with ideas? In that case, managers might really appreciate you offering constructive suggestions if you feel the writing there is outmoded or simply doesn't work as it should.

So, how could your writing actually help improve things? Streamlining communication could be a quick win. Busy bosses dread information overload: people constantly seeking direction and copying them in unnecessarily to lengthy, disordered missives. They're too busy to sift through data. Conversely, they also hate having too little information to make informed decisions.

Imagine for example, a manager has asked an employee how they plan to write up the minutes of a meeting held earlier that day. The employee e-mails back:

'I'll be recording what everyone says and then writing this up afterwards, for circulation to all who attended. I hope you find this helpful.'

That's certainly concise writing but it's not effective. How much more helpful to the manager would be a considered, structured response along the lines:

'I propose to:

- write up all material points;
- indicate what items were closed (needing no further action);
- indicate what actions are ongoing, and who does what, when;
- write an action plan and ensure everyone who needs to know does – which may be more than just the people who attended the meeting.'

Understand your strengths in thinking through the brief; your ideas, your disruptiveness (in the sense of innovating change for the better!) and write with structured points aimed at producing a good end result. It's a habit you can easily slip into.

On a practical writing level, too many exclamation marks and emojis may not go down too well, even if the organization sees this as acceptable amongst peers. Different emojis work better for some cultures than others, and do be aware that some colleagues or clients (for example some people on the autism spectrum) may struggle to identify expressions in emojis. The right words work far better for them.

Also, some cultures and organizations will actually see emojis as entirely off limits. Check what's acceptable where you work or plan to work.

Very importantly, never forget that respectful language pays dividends across all scenarios.

CASE STUDY   Bringing people along on the journey

Here's a real-life e-mail exchange from a boss in a major international company to a junior member of staff, recruited a couple of months before.

> Boss: 'So, how's it going? What's the dream?'

> Employee: 'To have lots of data.'

> Boss: 'Oh, that sounds like a nightmare to me. What are you going to do with the data?'

> Employee: 'That's a tricky one. I'm going to have to go away and think about that.'

The very next week she e-mailed over:

> 'I've analysed the data so far and we need to drive results in...' (she then highlighted a specific area).

She had cut through the noise, as requested, to deliver positive action.

She was pleased and her boss was pleased. The communication exchange had worked for both. The boss had motivated the employee by highlighting her expertise, admitting that was not his skillset. He guided her by highlighting how to focus. He needed data not just to produce information but to gain knowledge on which to build results. Together they delivered. That's how you bring people along on the journey via writing effectively.

When you're the boss, writing brings extra challenges!

Accessible, inclusive language that says the right things brings people on board, as we saw in the Nationwide case study. Time after time, simple can be smart. It's easy for each of us to forget that! It's definitely time to ditch any 'I'm cleverer than you' obfuscation. I'm using the inaccessible-to-many word '*obfuscation*' to make a point. Your business English is not clever if people don't readily understand it, across cultures and generations.

As a boss, you're at the stage of your career where you should know that confusing and reader-unfriendly messages can = lost profits + lost sales and/or custom + loss of professionalism + lost goodwill. Beyond this, you need to be credible so people will trust what you say and what you do.

You also need to:

- inspire and grow your people;
- encourage ideas and interaction;
- identify talent and strengths, develop teams accordingly;
- listen and learn;
- communicate values and strategy;
- persuade – and get great results;
- know how to communicate good and bad news effectively.

It's a tall order!

It's taken time and effort recruiting, you've got to see it through: your employees need to see writing that makes them feel valued, through the good times and the bad.

Make the workplace as enjoyable an experience as you can. Deliver the promise you made when you attracted them. In terms of your business writing, check your messages align with their goals alongside yours. Writing becomes more about the 'we' than simply the 'I'. You'll find you get people on board much more easily by reframing (as just one example): '*You must do this*' to '*We all need this to work because...*' and give the reasons why such action must happen.

Have you got a corporate writing style guide in place? Should you? This is a brave new business world we're entering and you ignore the importance of written word power at your peril!

Spontaneous positive e-mails from bosses can act as a figurative pat on the back, such as:

'That was a job well done. Keep up the good work.'

'You made great use of your strong negotiating skills there!'

'I'm delighted to report to shareholders that it's the teams' consistent efforts during difficult trading conditions that have brought about these improved results.'

This writing can really bolster morale and make employees feel valued.

If something has not gone so well, a timely e-mail from a manager can still be viewed positively by employees, for example:

'Yes, that was a tricky scenario – one to learn from another time. If something like it arises again, it could be ideal to contact (name of colleague with experience) for their advice.'

This latter example demonstrates the manager's empathy for the difficult situation the employee has faced and also offers positive guidance on a likely solution for next time.

Stay up to date yourself. Check that the voice and tone of your writing also aligns with the other channels the organization uses. It's never a good idea, as a boss, to become a 'communication dinosaur' because you don't listen and learn too. It doesn't mean you have to go the other extreme though, with overly casual sentences, such as:

'Why did you do that, huh?'

'Get with the power words, pal!'

'Gravitas' matters: it signifies the respect earned by serious intelligence. It's a power word one 20-something client identified to me as being an essential characteristic in a boss. I agree that managers' writing needs to show both gravitas and authority, to earn staff's respect and trust in what the managers are communicating. If you are to lead, people need to know why they should follow, and why being proactive will take everyone forward. Effective writing helps do just that.

Effective writing blends disciplines and departments

All too often, we see departments or disciplines within larger organizations compete with each other in their written communication. You sometimes wouldn't believe they work for the same outfit. Have you come across this?

My advice is simple: appreciate what each brings to the table, pool your writing strengths and see how you will strengthen your teams. All need to pull together, to see as one: 'what's the true commercial purpose of what we write?'

Here's a writing exercise I use in my workshops that brings people together in a surprising way.

I ask attendees (from differing professional disciplines) to imagine they have to write a set of instructions for a new entrant to the workplace. It's about how to make a cup of tea, with no vending machine to hand. Just jot some ideas down now, before reading on.

It's fascinating to see the differing approaches. Those of a technical persuasion tend to start the exercise by describing all the equipment and ingredients needed from the outset, then numbering each step in a logical sequence. Some focus on the health and safety aspect: once brewed, let your hot drink cool before tasting. Marketers often wax lyrical on making the event an experience: they routinely suggest adding a slice of chocolate cake, then relaxing and seeing how the ideas flow!

Then at the end, I ask attendees to read out their instructions and we take a vote on the 'best bits', which would then be adopted as best practice, were the instructions ever needed.

Analysing differing styles of writing, then choosing the aspects that appeal to all, really brings people together. Naturally, tea drinking may not be part of your office culture, so consider adapting this exercise to one that would yield helpful interaction.

Writing across generations in your customer base

The tips I have given so far will help you write successfully across your multigenerational client base too. One style of writing won't suit all. Look at how your target audience writes, not just in cultural terms but in generational terms too, and mirror it as far as is valid to do so, without losing your professional authenticity.

Your checklist for action

Your writing is likely to succeed if:

- you allow it to evolve but also remember that it needs to appeal to, and be understood by, all the generations in your audience;
- your values are readily visible and consistent throughout – and promote the likelihood of a good work environment/employee experience;
- you use the right channels and the right language, for you and your readers;
- you use powerful words that engage, energize and persuade;
- you recognize when gravitas matters;
- you manage expectations regarding timescales in all work projects (including continuously keeping people in the loop during recruitment processes).

Your writing is likely to fail if:

- you can't engage your target audience in generational, as well as cultural terms;

- you don't respond in sharpish time frames when expected;
- your lack of interaction comes over as disrespectful;
- you don't recognize when flippancy is inappropriate;
- your writing lacks structure and direction.

05
Telling your story through social media

Social media has shaken 'the rules' of business writing

Just as the printing press revolutionized the way written communication could spread messages far and wide, so social media has turned the business world and traditional writing inside out.

I'll talk you through how social media requires an integrated approach – and a distinctly conversational writing style that comes naturally to younger generations but often less so for more traditional writers. So in this chapter, there will be some line-by-line analysis, but we'll also immerse ourselves in the fuller picture to see how the social media 'storyline' fits together.

Get into the social media mindset

From the simple sharing of a message to in-depth conversation, to following the latest news, to opening transactions and closing deals, social media is an intrinsic part of our world. Incidentally, I'm describing 'social media' as a collective singular here, in the sense of the activity on social media. Grammatically, it would also be correct to write that social media 'are' part of our world.

If you can write well, not only are you improving your career prospects generally, you can also deal with any social media, where the written word takes centre stage. What you need to write depends on your personal and company story, the points you want to make, the goals you need to achieve, and how you write to attract and maintain readers' interaction with you, as the story evolves.

This chapter is about getting you involved in the social media mindset.

Get your business message to anyone, anywhere, anytime

It's all about sharing information and collaborating online, bringing the facility to enable everyone to get in touch with anyone, anywhere, anytime. In business, although the biggest players have the biggest budget, they can't get complacent. Even the smallest voice now has a megaphone to communicate globally, be part of the conversation – and go viral.

Responsive companies of all sizes know the importance of effective online presence on social media where written content is king. Even the very best visuals rarely work by themselves: it's usually the captions and descriptions that ultimately sell the messages. Infographics can be immensely valuable, almost at a glance, via thought-through visuals aided by writing that imparts key information interestingly and concisely.

People constantly check their networks, so content needs to be updated: they want to be kept posted on things such as helpful information, breaking news, innovation, events, offers, etc.

Written content also needs to be suitable for mobile devices and smart watches. Users who are 'on the go', maybe waiting for a train or between meetings, need easily highlighted messages and to know at a glance where you're leading. The original 'click here' has given way to the (hopefully) more enticing 'read more'.

We see social media used alongside, sometimes in place of, traditional leaflets or mailing. Words even take centre stage in the fast-growing messaging via video. Every message has been (or should have been) finely crafted by that business. Being social offers the opportunity (and expectation) to talk not just about brand, products and services but also to introduce personalities: the people behind the brand. There's more opportunity for storytelling that resonates and a huge demand for customized messages to elicit buy-in or positive reaction. The word power skills system shown in Chapter 2 is immensely valuable, as the challenge (and the exciting part) is how to get your words heard through the noise. How to adapt, to keep up with the trends – and even create them.

English has such an advantage, being used extensively across multiple platforms. But if English isn't your company's first language or that of your social media writers, remember points earlier in the book. Words that are right for your home market may not work abroad, even where English is the common language.

As an example, let's look at this wording on sportswear brand Adidas' global website:

> Go get better, share your skills, compare yourself with the best and challenge your friends.

It uses very clear wording, easily understandable on first reading. Let's contrast this with wording used on their Adidas India website:

> Criticism and self-doubt can paralyze the most talented athletes. Only a rare breed converts the stones thrown at them into milestones...

The language is rather more poetic and thought provoking. It requires a more sophisticated understanding of the English used.

Coca-Cola is one of the most recognized global brands and it too adapts the English it uses across the world. So although we see the social media hashtag #PerfectCoke globally, some countries won't necessarily understand #SwelterStopper used for ice-cool Coke or #SarapNgFirst – 'the first time taste of the #PerfectCoke experience'. This latter example purposefully features Tagalog English to resonate with their target youth market in the Philippines.

If you decide to outsource any of your social media (especially likely if you export), or if you simply collaborate with other partners, don't forget you are ultimately accountable for the messages you put out. One charity found this out to their cost, despite their best intentions:

CASE STUDY   Samaritans charity

Samaritans are a highly respected UK charity, offering support to anyone in emotional distress.

Looking for ways of helping vulnerable people online (especially those aged 18–35), they hired a digital agency to help them launch the #SamaritansRadar app. This sent an alert to users when people they followed posted messages that algorithms picked up to suggest depressed or suicidal thoughts.

The app was withdrawn almost immediately after attracting criticism that it didn't work. It certainly failed on a semantic level, as one Twitter user showed. He added the #SamaritansRadar hashtag to his innocuous post: 'Making a mixtape of smooth jazz classics. Maybe I should end it all with a bit of Alfonzo Blackwell. #SamaritansRadar.'

The algorithm had mistakenly picked up on the words 'maybe I should end it all' as alluding to suicide.

What are the key objectives?

These include: engage, be shared and convert – by being relevant, useful, knowledgeable, credible, consistently professional and personable. All your corporate communications need to reflect your values and your personality – and achieve your goals.

It's not in the scope of this book to cover writing for websites or search engine optimization (SEO) in any detail. But it's important to know that the algorithms of Google and other search engines look out for certain signals (that may change over time). Your focus always has to be about creating good-quality content and coherence between your website and your communication off that platform, including social media posts. How engaging both are affects your visibility and could impact on your SEO ranking. Google's guidelines for SEO state that pages must be written primarily for users, not for search engines: '#1: Focus on the user and all else will follow' and this rings true for social media generally.

Beyond that you will need:

- a clear structure that's easy to read;
- useful links that add value to the text (that is, don't link for the sake of it);
- to engage social signals that are likely to improve your visibility.

Social signals mean the interaction your website and social media posts are gaining (visits, likes, shares, dialogue, etc). It's about realizing that you're no longer just broadcasting, you need to be part of a conversation – and a listener too. When everyone is an author, make sure you're generating content that's valued. Write things of interest, offer value, project a brand that engages, get involved – and show you're interested too.

Look at this Facebook offer from Pizza Express (fast-food company).

CASE STUDY   Create your new favourite pizza

Pizza Express posted a Facebook offer, inviting diners to join them in celebrating their new Spring menu. Their enticement was: 'create your own pizza to feature on our Autumn menu.'

The winning pizza would join the favourites on their menu and '£10,000 AND a holiday for two to the Amalfi Coast could all be yours!'

Emblazoned at the side of the page was: 'Free Dough Balls for every entry!', ie every entrant is actually a winner.

The success of the offer is in the result and they were instantly eliciting positive interaction, such as: 'Thanks/Cheers/BIG THANKS!!/A fairly amazing prize bundle, and a fun competition too! They've done a really nice job with that competition...'

Let's analyse the components of their successful writing:

1 There was a compelling headline that appealed to the individual reader.

2 There was a great offer – not just the chance of the 'fairly amazing prize bundle' as one reader put it, but also a freebie for every entrant.

3 For discoverability, the tags were 'holiday' and 'Pizza Express'.

4 There was also a link to their website and Pizza Express deals.

Look out for examples for yourself. See what you feel works, and you're sure to find writing that:

- expresses key messages in the right channel, in language that's right for the expectations, needs, aspirations and interests of the target audience on that platform (casual/more formal/culture/right for that generation, etc?);

- has compelling headlines that attract target readers' attention (more on this shortly);

- communicates even complex messages simply (links can take readers to detail needed);

- maintains interest and credibility (readers must trust you to know links will take them to something professional/of value, otherwise why click?);

- is current (you can refresh useful content, as I'll show shortly).

Your business objectives are usually any or all of the following:

- to increase brand awareness and 'be part of a conversation' (as positively as possible);

- to get your messages across and, depending on your business, to boost sales;

- to create ongoing dialogue, listen to customers and improve;
- to gain market insights;
- to share valuable information, develop and maintain relationships;
- to get your messages found widely through SEO.

Keep up with the major platforms out there

Businesses need to choose the channels that best suit their needs – and also those of their target demographic. Current leaders include Facebook, YouTube, WhatsApp, Facebook Messenger, Snapchat, WeChat, Instagram, QZone and Twitter. Keep up to date, as platforms constantly change.

Then, you can't just expect everyone to open, let's say, a Facebook or Twitter account in order to engage with you. Choose channels you know your audience is interested in too (and remember that not everyone wants to be on the same channel. Currently, Facebook is losing upcoming generations in vast numbers, as they don't want to be on the same platform as their elders!). Be prepared to invest time in getting social, otherwise how can you expect to create a loyal following or generate leads?

As more channels get added to the mix, recognize and adapt to their style. Keep your purpose in mind and be clear.

How do companies shine through their social media interaction?

There's been a shift in focus from product or service (the focus of traditional writing) to consumer in social media. So writing must be:

- reader-focused and less about direct selling (this doesn't completely rule out selling, depending on what each channel allows in terms of promotion);
- more about your voice and brand personality.

Share information and experiences of value, the newest this, the helpful that, etc. If people value your content, they can become 'brand advocates', without ever meeting you. You're likely to reciprocate, opening up new dialogues and horizons.

Learn by looking at how companies shine through their online interaction. This case study highlights how one company succeeds.

CASE STUDY   Innocent Drinks

Innocent Drinks started off as a fairly small UK soft drinks company in 1998. Known not just for their drinks but also for their 'quirky' offline and online brand presentation, they built up an impressive following. This attracted the interest of the giant Coca-Cola company, who took ownership in 2013 and pledged commitment to the original company ethos and the Innocent Charity Foundation, funded by a percentage of profits.

At the time of writing, Innocent have an enviable 596,983 Facebook page likes – achieved, I think, not only through their products but also through their positive and reactive customer interaction.

If we look at their social media feeds, they often use the same content across channels. Keeping it innovative, current and something that they wanted people to share, the founders devised a #chainofgood compliment generator. They posted this on their blog and Facebook page, introducing it with a strapline about their product: 'tastes good, does you good, does others good.' A short write-up described how their drinks have natural goodness, and how a percentage of profits go to charity.

Visitors to the #chainofgood were invited to choose and post a compliment from the 'compliment generator' such as 'You are a walking high-five' (50,000 shares). The element of choice meant the words were right for their readers' readers too. They also invited suggestions, to enhance appeal and interaction. The overall effect was to spread positive brand awareness. Keeping current and relevant, the company adapted the generator for occasions, such as downloadable cards for Mother's Day, complete with company logo.

The style in the following tweet is a million miles away from the Innocent approach. It's sent by a 'social media' company as their standard 'first point of contact' tweet, to all people they have started following on Twitter:

@ (name of person they follow) Do you blog?

Would it surprise you that no one appears to reply? It's abrupt (which is different to being concise) and doesn't show any interest in the person they question. One gets the feeling that the company tweets only so they can sell their blogging services.

Writing that creates trust can create a community

Building a community through social media is not just for commercial brands. We now find many more social enterprises setting up, not just in traditional third sector activity areas such as health and social care, education and community services, but also in traditional private sector activities. Most encouragingly, we see companies who want to use their profits for the public good.

Charismatic retail magnate Theo Paphitis is one such supporter of skills and entrepreneurship. The following case study shows how he created a supportive small business community via social media.

CASE STUDY Theo Paphitis' Small Business Sunday community

In common with many highly successful entrepreneurs, Theo Paphitis is open about his dyslexia, which has actually afforded him an advantage in understanding the importance of simple, vibrant, well-chosen words to sell messages, products and services and create a following.

He realized how helpful it would be to small businesses in the UK (known to be the lifeblood of the economy), to understand that writing with impact on social media – via professional, mobile-friendly devices and websites – was a powerful tool for networking and growth.

To this end, he created Small Business Sunday (shortened to the hashtag #SBS on Twitter). Each week, he rewards small businesses that tweet him @TheoPaphitis and write about their businesses in one tweet (with hashtag #SBS) in a dedicated time slot, on a Sunday. He then retweets his favourite lucky six, judged on how well they have communicated their message. As he has over 490,000 followers, this provides them with a massive publicity boost.

Theo continues to build this #SBS community not only with offers and by staging events for winners, but also by providing a website for interaction within the community itself. He and his group of companies actively get involved in the conversation.

In his words:

> My vision is that everyone who has ever won an #SBS re-tweet from me becomes part of a friendly club. Like-minded individuals can share successes and learnings... I know I have been lucky in business and I am keen now to spread goodwill to others, of course not forgetting that very often you make your own luck by making use of every opportunity.

This and similar cases are very exciting applications of business English writing in today's workplace. Can you see how, where English is a common language, such skilful use of social media to build communities can be rolled out – not simply on a local basis but nationally and internationally too? We saw in Chapter 4 how strongly upcoming generations feel about 'putting something back' into the world. It's a great trend for all to embrace.

The long and the short of it: past, present and future

It's not just short posts that can go viral. Now 'everyone is a writer' – but not everyone is willing or able to write good material in depth. Articles with detailed information can be highly valuable.

Digital Storytelling has become a big focus of online marketing and aims at encouraging user-generated content (UGC). Naturally you must write the right information so people find your posts. Without discoverability, you won't get shared! So provide the right links, photos, etc.

Your stories can be brief but sometimes it's the detail that makes them come alive. That's the beauty of being able to provide a link in your short post to a fuller article on your website or elsewhere.

As part of the story, consider intriguing your readers – maybe hold some information back, so they want to explore further. A link can take them to that valuable 'more'. But avoid 'clickbait' – the pejorative term to describe captivating links that only take you to spam advertisements, etc.

CASE STUDY   Ogilvy and Mather

Ogilvy and Mather, the most awarded advertising agency in the world, intersperse old and new content, and long and short blogs/articles, to create and retain interest.

They embrace the iconic status of their founder, original 'Mad Man' David Ogilvy. His words of 1982 still ring true: 'People who think well, write well. Woolly minded people write woolly memos, woolly letters and woolly speeches.'

The agency regularly posts his quotes on their website, Facebook page and Twitter feed. They routinely mix and match language of the past with today's, as this Facebook 'Ogilvyism' post shows:

Disruption of convention. Disruption of rules. Disruption of received wisdom. Disruption of 'we've always done it this way'.

#ThoughtLeadership #Inspire

They then provide a link to a much fuller and perennially valuable 'years-old article' by David Ogilvy, on the importance of stimulating creativity and innovation, through information and reflection.

The important thing is that all your posts work towards a common goal. Are you going to post similar material across the platforms you use? Whatever you do, the messages need to harmonize.

> **Activity:** It's not just the big players who can seize an opportunity to link new posts to the history of success their company has built. Can you rejig a good past post of yours, to make it relevant today?
>
> Are there tips you can share, even re-share? The principles of great communication work across channels, even across time.

Further writing tips for key channels such as Facebook, Twitter and LinkedIn

Facebook

Facebook is currently the world's largest social networking site and so offers enormous potential for going viral. You may consider this a strong case for using global rather than local English (see Chapter 6).

When writing a company Facebook page, create relationships with users. Show you are there to do business with them. Be interesting;

offer something to attract visitors to your page and get them to hit 'Like' – a visible approval of a product or service.

Writing tips to help are:

- Be authentic, let readers see your personality, on a professional basis.

- Keep personal comments for your personal accounts, have a corporate policy for Facebook, Instagram posts, etc.

- Ask fans/'likers' for feedback on your product/services via questions in posts, or links to surveys.

- Post good news on your business: sector-specific general updates; insightful, people-based anecdotes about your organization; only use humour that will work for your audience/culture.

- Share YouTube video clips and other visuals, of general interest as well as about your business.

- Reply to comments. Thank people for positive comments and post promptly with your viewpoint, to counter any negative comments.

Many of you will have passed on a positive message about a company to others and, in a sense, become an unpaid advocate of their brand. Take a look at the language they used that engaged your interest. It's a fascinating exercise that can help your writing.

Twitter

Twitter is a real-time information network where you simply find the accounts you find most compelling and follow the conversations.

Each short burst of information is called a tweet. Limited to 280 characters, it's about expressing key points concisely. Photos, video and other links can add to the story.

Tips for businesses writing on Twitter include the tips I've given for Facebook, as well as:

- Algorithms prove that content that's helpful gets found and shared. So write tips/hacks on things that work or problems to avoid, inspirational quotes, universal truths, or something relating to a trending topic, etc.

- You can actively ask people to share your information: 'please share' or 'please retweet' can work for good content.

- Analyse which tweets are getting retweeted or 'favourited'.

- Post your tweets in the right time zone for your potential global readers. Twitter is fast-moving and transient, so re-post tweaked tweets at differing intervals – and double-check for mistakes before you post. Speed can trap you into making them!

- Hashtags are useful for introducing topics of general interest and are searchable, for example #BusinessCommunication or #globalprojects.

- The name you write under (your 'Twitter handle') and your Twitter bio can provide an opportunity to describe what you do and/or your brand (mine is @wordpowerskills – do say hello!).

Where writers err is when the message is all about *them* and nothing to do with others. What do you think of this tweet sent to me as a direct message (DM)?

> Hey what do you do? I deliver strategic digital transformation. Come over and like my Facebook page!

If you have written a good bio, complete with your website details, any tweet writer should have the courtesy to read the outline of what you do, before making contact in this way. This tweet is actually only about them. And would you talk to this person so directly, without introduction or further evidence, in any other business situation? Also, they can't assume the reader will be on Facebook.

As social media is about writing for people, not robots – and will continue to be, even in an age of increasing artificial intelligence (AI) – it requires accessible, conversational language. I think tweet 2 below generally works better for the medium than tweet 1:

1 There's little doubt about it, it feels rather good that my business writing book appears to be useful as it's selling.

2 Woohoo, so pleased: my book is in the #businesswriting charts because it helps! Thank you so much! #lovemyreaders

But if the style is too effusive for your target audience, don't use it. Use your judgement – and, as I mention throughout, it's a must to have a policy on language that's off limits, eg expletives or religious/political/sexist/racist comments.

Remember also that people use Twitter to make immediate complaints. If your company is involved, be sure to monitor for them and deal with them quickly. Others will be watching how you deal with this too.

Don't forget, the various platforms actively want you to use them. Take advantage of their specific tips on what works best at any given time. Twitter Business for example, currently offers a Twitter Content Strategy to help you write what they consider compelling posts optimized for their platform.

Newsletters, blogs, vlogs or microblog posts

Newsletters and blogs read like articles and inform. Whilst printed newsletters and other material have to explain background within the articles themselves, online newsletters, blogs, vlogs (video logs) or microblogs (such as Twitter posts) can easily refer to detailed information elsewhere online. Post regularly to keep material fresh and build up a readership that you hope will be loyal advocates.

Keep your paragraphs shorter than in print (some recommend four sentences maximum). As reading on a computer screen can be tiring, and reading on mobile devices can be 'on the go', you need to 'grab eyeballs' so people do read. Invite questions and comments (and add reply buttons) – as long as you plan to respond to these. Get involved with others' blogs too. Be discoverable and maintain visibility.

CASE STUDY   Richard Branson and the Virgin Group

Sir Richard Branson, the highly successful founder of the Virgin Group, is known for his inspirational blogs. He gives valuable advice in one of his posts as a LinkedIn Influencer, on how he manages to write and avoid writer's block:

> What do you talk to your friends about? What was that interesting article you read the other day? What was everyone chatting about in the office at lunch? Could there be a blog in that? More than likely, yes.

He advises keeping it personal, as inauthenticity is easy to sniff out. If it wasn't really him writing on LinkedIn or posting his virgin.com blogs, people would spot it a mile off. He loves sharing what's happening in his world and the latest happenings at Virgin, and can think of no better way of doing it than in real time, online.

If we analyse his blogs, they are often very short. One blog simply read: 'The difference is in the difference'. That sums up his philosophy that if you aren't making and expressing a difference then you shouldn't be in business.

He then asks for readers' comments on the business difference they are trying to achieve. His words 'I'd love to hear about it' show his interest and encourage interaction: the hallmark of successful social media writing.

This short blog (tags: inspiration, business, quotes) achieved 11,100 shares, with a breakdown: 687 Facebook likes, 3,186 Tweets, 2,100 Google+ and 5,100 LinkedIn shares. There are also links to: 'My Top 10 Quotes on Leadership' and 'My Top 10 Quotes on Failure'.

So if we analyse his writing:

1 he often uses an intriguing headline;
2 he writes simple, universal truths expressed in his easy, conversational style, reinforced by personal brand;
3 his business messages reach out to an inclusive 'you';
4 there's a call to action in an engaged style.

We see this mix of easy language elsewhere on Virgin websites, for example in their Help forums – 'Settle in and get comfy, we'd love to see you get involved' – as part of how customers experience the brand.

Virgin never ignore the business of selling. In all posts, we still see traditional calls to action such as 'Sign up to our newsletter', 'Hurry!', 'Online exclusive offer' or 'Don't miss out'.

It's not surprising people love sharing this advice, as it takes the fear away from the task. Don't let nervousness block the vitality of your business writing.

LinkedIn and SlideShare

LinkedIn is a networking site for matters strictly related to business and careers, etc. Blatant selling of products or services is disallowed. But employers do trawl for new talent on it, so write a great profile, showcasing your attributes (whether as a provider or seeker), so it can double up as a résumé/CV. Avoid words that LinkedIn identify as clichés (more on this in Chapter 11).

Use LinkedIn's dynamic extra features to help you project 'brand you' and make yourself discoverable. Start with a headline that sums up who you are and what you want.

Here are some fictitious examples:

1 Bart Wierks – Improving IT Systems * Seeking Career Opportunity.

2 Carl Chapman – Change Management Guru 'Hire me and results guaranteed'.

3 Monica Heiss – Senior Associate at XYZ Global Staffing Associates * 4,000 connections.

In example 1, we see at a glance what Bart does and what he's seeking. In example 2, Carl uses rather more expressive language. His words express his personal brand and self-belief. In example 3, Monica feels that her position and her networking credentials speak for themselves. Which style, if any, do you think works best? How would you write?

Do also consider posting your own interesting content on SlideShare, a LinkedIn company that's the world's largest professional content sharing platform. It's a great way of getting noticed professionally.

What excites people so much they want to share it?

You already have an idea about this and indeed, analysing across all channels, these messages get shared most:

- Lists and tips – especially things on how to work better, for example, 'How Successful People Stay Calm'; 'The Three Qualities of People I Most Enjoy Working With'; 'Ten Top Tips for Leadership'.

- Articles that bring out an emotional response – positive emotions get a faster response on most channels, eg greatest, happiest, cutest, wow this is GREAT! That doesn't mean that negative emotions don't work, however. 'Four Destructive Myths to Banish' definitely gets shared. 'Do you know how many things you could be sued for?' will most likely work better for an insurer than 'We introduce our exciting new insurance product!' But choose your negatives carefully in a business context.

- Quotes – as with articles, people share emotions just as much (maybe more) than they share facts. Share others' words of wisdom or witticisms, etc, and you can become part of the chatter. If the quotes are your own, you may have more influence – and lead the conversation.

- Verbs – whether knowledge- or action-based, for example: know, prove, think, grab one now, hurry, don't miss out.

- Captivating captions/slogans that underpin and enhance a relevant and brilliant visual/picture/video – for example:

o Apple: *Think different*

o Nike: *Just do it*

o KitKat: *Have a break… have a KitKat*

(Just listen to the sound of the 'k' in the KitKat slogan. You can almost hear the sound of the biscuit breaking! That's effective writing.) Alliteration can also help engagement – for brands such as PayPal, Coca-Cola, Dunkin' Donuts as well as for articles or videos: 'Colloquialisms Can Confuse'.

- Posts with calls to action (more on this shortly).
- Facts and infographics.

See how Step 3 in the word power skills system in Chapter 2 – 'Make the right impact' – will help you greatly here.

When online, you might like to check how global media company Buzzfeed Inc. master digital sharing of 'the most social content on the web'. Notice how they customize the home page for the country, eg United States, Australia, India, etc. Get a feel for what might work for you. But don't lift copy or images and use them as your own or you could face plagiarism charges.

Call people to action – and check it's worked

An important element of social media is checking that it worked. If you go unnoticed, it might as well be money down the drain. So it never harms to hammer home this message: build in effective calls to action as if your life depended on it. You want people to react. Better, you want them to discuss positively, even evangelize. Mostly in business we need buy-in and sales. Ogilvy and Mather aren't afraid to state: 'We sell or else'.

Express, where feasible, what you want people to do next, *in all your written tasks*. Your focus in social media may be selling messages about brand, but you can still hope to convert to sales at a later date. Invite readers to subscribe to your newsletter or contact you. You can ask people:

- to *share* some piece of content (industry insights, other knowledge, observations, news, your own tips, etc) or your brand;
- to *like* on Facebook; or
- to *retweet* what you say (evangelism can achieve sales too).

The hard fact is that without sales and profits, your core business can flounder.

Tips for writing calls to action

- Explain why (one or more major benefits) and how people should respond.
- Communicate clearly what customers will get.
- Offer a realistic deadline and the benefits for the customer of acting quickly (a free offer/discount/upgrade/limited edition/pegged interest rates, etc).
- Highlight dates or events that can be useful to your demographic. The more national, multicultural or international you become or want to become, the more hooks you can use, eg Christmas, Sinterklaas, Thanksgiving, Diwali, etc.
- By showing you understand issues of relevance to the world out there (where your current and prospective clients reside) you can become the trusted friend that they will turn to for advice. Once they see that your advice comes from a place of values and knowledge, they are more likely to pay for targeted advice from 'that trusted friend' – or at least be an advocate for you to others.

Don't 'overthink' when you write. Don't lose sight of the essence of your business that needs to be written throughout your business, from your business cards on!

Your social media posts need to cross-refer to your website

Your website needs to act as a hub for your social media posts. All content should cross-refer and have a consistent look, feel and corporate style as part of the reader experience. So, just as with your social media posts, do your messages stand out with the 'power words' that reflect your values? Was your website originally written in a traditional style? Just as it had to be adapted for mobile devices, might it have to be further adapted to align with how you write for social media?

Now people expect bite-sized messages, headlined and sub-headlined to break up text for scan reading. Captions too have a role to play in explaining the visuals you use. Make everything discoverable.

Finally, if your website is in English, do you use this in a global or local context? With the potential to reach out to new territories via social media too, writing effectively in English means one size won't fit all.

Telling your story

We've looked at many examples of how companies project their voice and personality in social media and how they tell their brand story, drawing readers into it and being interested in readers' stories too.

By now you should have a definite idea of what story you have to tell, alongside your company's personality. It's your exciting challenge to write vibrant content that draws people towards you.

So what's *your* compelling story? What did it begin with? Where are you at? Where are you going? Are you going to let readers share your people's stories and see their personalities? And are you going to invite your audience to share their stories?

There are no rights and wrongs here. This approach may not work for all but it allows you to understand principles behind the mindset required in writing for social media. As a checklist we could add:

- Never lose sight of your objectives and your readers' needs and expectations.

- How will you adapt your tone for the demographic (sector, culture, generation) you target?

- How will you get them to respond?

- How will you maintain interaction, as positively as possible?

- Are you asking the right questions? Are you getting the answers you hope for?

- Who will be there to respond to their questions – or their complaints, if any? (In social media, people expect rapid response.)

- How could your communication better lead to building the community you desire?

This chapter has shown you how companies write for these social media platforms for different reasons. They are largely to do with a desire to get individuals to help them get their name out there, even go viral, to develop and maintain a good global reputation. Just as a company needs to be responsive to customers when writing for social media, it needs to respond by revising corporate writing generally, as times move on. Just as business writing expressions such as 'hereunder', 'the aforesaid', 'we remain your obedient servants' and so on have been ditched over the past few decades, companies need to identify what becomes currently mainstream. Language evolves so policies need to as well, otherwise, once again, widely differing corporate styles can confuse readers and work against brand.

Everything has to be consummately professional because reputation matters – and it's easy for inferior writing to go viral for all the wrong reasons!

Your checklist for action

- How do you plan to write for social media? What are your objectives? Which channels will you use?

- How are you going to communicate your personality, as well as your values?

- Design writing that is discoverable by and relevant to your target audience.

- Be social when you write; get involved and maintain interaction, so that you create a following/community and benefit from loyal brand advocates.

- Don't see social media writing as an inferior form of business communication; be professional and mind your and others' reputation. Mistakes can rapidly go viral.

- Check that everyone in your company, as well as in any outside agency you hire, understands how to project your voice: sometimes personal, always corporate.

- Keep up with emerging channels; tailor your writing and formatting for readers' business and cultural expectations.

- Analyse the language used in posts that work (these can be others' posts, not just your own); adapt your vocabulary and understand that language evolves.

- Ensure that your message is consistent across all your communication channels.

- Use the word power skills writing system as it will continue to work across emerging channels too.

06
Standard or variant English?

It's strange how a lot of businesses don't actually define what they mean by business English. It can be a must if you work in a multicultural team, a cosmopolitan office, a multinational organization, or have a potential global reach through social media.

So let's get specific. We know English is a major language of commercial communication and a world language of the internet and of global access to knowledge, spoken by around a quarter of the world's population! When we use the term 'business English' though, it's a generic term used for dealing with business communication in English. You may still have to design communication that specifically covers the many variants you'll encounter.

'Standard' and 'variant' English

Globally there are actually more non-native speakers of English than native English speakers. It belongs to no single culture but acts as a bridge across borders and cultures.

When I first worked abroad, I saw how multinationals wanted to seize the competitive edge in their use of English as a global business language. It was then that I realized how puzzled both foreigners and native English speakers can be by the way English is so often used. Sometimes it's because non-native English speakers use it in unconventional ways. Sometimes it's because people don't realize that UK English differs from the many other variations of business English that exist. These include US or American English, Australian English, Caribbean English, Indian English, Singapore English and South African English. It's an extensive list. Business communication is crucial to success. So if people are puzzled by it, this is bad news. Getting the right messages out and receiving the right answers are the lifeblood of commercial success. I found it helped my clients communicate effectively cross-culturally by following some norms of 'standard' English. The result? People understood each other!

So what is 'standard' English? I use it to mean the English routinely described in mainstream English dictionaries and grammar books. It's the English used throughout this book, likely to be understood by all users.

Unless I indicate otherwise, the spelling and grammar used are the UK English variety requested by my publishers, to follow their house style. One of the challenges in writing UK English is that there can be more than one correct way of spelling certain words, as I've mentioned earlier. For example: recognize and recognise, judgment and judgement, e-mail and email can all be used correctly in UK English. Some people give explanations for these differences that are too simplistic, saying that 'recognize' indicates a US English spelling. But this is only part of the picture – and you will find more on variant spellings later in the book.

At times I refer to US English as well, where there are clearly divergent spellings or meanings. But the book won't address differences between UK and US English in detail. The important thing is: know that you need to check.

This takes me to my next point. Whenever we write and whatever we write, we must understand the conventions to follow, if we are to please our target readers. If necessary, explain at the outset the convention you are following, so you can avoid unfounded or unnecessary criticism. One thing is sure: if someone can find grounds for criticizing writing, they will! Be one step ahead and, if you are asked, understand which variant you're using and why.

Be consistent, to underpin a strong, quality-conscious corporate image. You undermine this if some people in your company use UK English spellcheck and grammar check and others use US English versions in their communication. I see this done all the time, simply because no one has bothered to issue professional corporate guidelines.

Writing for both native and non-native English speakers

You'll have noticed that when I refer to native English speakers this means anyone who speaks any variety of English as their first language.

If you're a non-native English speaker, you may know these categories: English as an acquired language (EAL), English as a foreign language (EFL), English for speakers of other languages (ESOL) and English as a second language (ESL). The book is suitable for all and terms I use are:

- *native English (NE) speaker or writer* to mean someone whose first language is English, and native English (NE) writing to refer to their writing;

- *non-native English (non-NE) speaker or writer* to mean someone whose first language is not English, and non-native English (non-NE) writing to refer to their writing.

Some surprising problems with English for global business

As well as there being different varieties of English, there are, in effect, sub-varieties directly caused by mixing English with the language patterns of the native country. Examples are Chinglish (Chinese–English), Manglish (Malaysian–English) and Singlish (Singapore–English). The same phenomenon can happen in any language mix.

Sometimes this can lead to out-and-out mistranslations. Although users may understand what they mean, these can be unintentionally funny or unintelligible to the foreign reader, as the following real-life mistranslated signs show. I deliberately don't highlight the countries concerned as it would be unfair to single any out. These mistakes occur across the board!

- Sign over an information booth: Question Authority

- Sign in a maternity ward: No children allowed

- Sign in a restaurant: Customers who find our waitresses rude ought to see our manager

- In an airline ticket office: We take your bags and send them in all directions

- In a hotel lift/elevator: Please leave your values at the front desk

The point is: do address the problem (even get professional help if needed), and check that your messages say what you intend them to say, especially in a global context, to people at differing levels of proficiency in English.

Let's now look at a sample of anglicized words used in Western Europe. Expressions such as 'a parking' (UK English: a car park; US English: a parking lot) or 'presentation charts' (UK English and US English: presentation slides) are used predominantly in Germany as well as words such as 'handy' in continental Europe (UK English: mobile phone; US English: cell phone) or 'beamer' in France and elsewhere (UK English: projector). But if we are writing globally, by definition, we're not just writing for readers in one country.

If the vast majority of English speakers have no idea what these sorts of 'pseudo-anglicisms' mean, this can lead to unintended problems.

Define business English within your company

It's clearly in your interests to evaluate whether the terms you use really are understood by your target audience. Terms that are understood in Western Europe may not have the same currency in Asian markets and so on. Certain English-sounding words may have crept into your usage but it doesn't mean they are internationally recognized.

Share your findings throughout your company, to gain consensus on the business English you plan to use. Flag up any words you discover that may not have common currency.

If you have just started your career, you can impress your boss by doing this. You can make a difference, boost your prospects and help your organization shine.

Your checklist for action

- Do you communicate with a specific group of English users? Or are you likely to be communicating worldwide?

- Do you identify and then use a single type of English every time you write in English? Or do you need to vary it according to your target audience each time?

- Do you set your computer spellcheck and grammar check to the type(s) of English you use?

- If so, do you check that it doesn't default to US English spelling (unless that's your preferred variety)?

- Do you regularly check that the words you use are understood by your readers?

- When you don't understand a word, be confident and ask its meaning.

- Regularly feed back your findings to colleagues.

07
Writing globally? Or in multinational teams?

Looking at how you use English at work

It's useful to hold up a figurative mirror and evaluate as far as possible:

- how your readers see themselves;
- how you see yourself – and your organization;
- how you see your readers;
- how your readers may see you through your writing.

As the images may diverge, successful writing will aim to remove any distortions, bringing the four equally important images together into sharp, correct focus. It appreciates diversity and embraces the fact that different cultures communicate differently. If you're dealing with a particular country, research how to communicate with their culture. The varying channels of social media broaden this need further, as we saw in Chapter 5. Don't overlook the fact that multicultural teams may also be found in your home workplace. My advice will help here too.

In outline, it's true to say that a typical Western style of writing comes over as structured and fairly direct (that said, you may still encounter waffle: lots of words with no clear purpose!).

If we look at Asian cultures, we can find extremely polite, formal, self-effacing communication. It can be considered bad style to get to the point too quickly and rude to make points too directly. Such cultures are likely to have a stronger focus on introduction, setting a respectful tone, developing rapport, only then ending on the main points (which they may imply rather than express).

Do address the cultural writing style needed for each task. One size won't fit all.

Do your words say what you think they say?

Have you ever had to explain to readers: 'Oh, I didn't mean that'? If so, you won't be alone.

That's why major UK companies and government agencies, as well as smaller players, all call me in as a troubleshooter to check over their business writing for native readers too! Are their words (to internal and external customers, suppliers and in technical documents, etc) *really* saying what they want them to say? It's not just a plain English issue: it's also about adopting the right frame of mind to make the right connections with readers. Stand back – and see your writing from all angles. An undoubtedly well-intentioned writer in Australia didn't do this when advertising literacy classes, as the text of this poster shows:

Are you an adult that cannot read? If so, we can help you.

The moment you say 'I didn't mean that!' is the moment you realize that no, your writing isn't saying what you meant.

Converting thoughts into words, then into writing

We all face real challenges when communicating. How do we convert what we're thinking into words – and convey meaning precisely? Writing words down can bring additional problems. Will the words work on paper or on the screen, when we're not there to explain them?

The factors that can distort intended meanings can naturally be a far greater challenge for non-native speakers of English. Empathize with the extra step they have to take: translating their words from their native language into English before they write them down. So if you are a non-native English speaker a systematic approach like this can help:

1 Identify the thought effectively in your own language.

2 Translate it correctly from your own language into English.

3 You may then need to convert the thought captured in English into the correct *written* English word.

4 Then make sure that the 'correct written English word' is actually one that your readers will understand.

5 Having done all this, your English writing should enable readers to respond the way you want. That's what you are in business for!

Let's see how we can all minimize any further distortions from planning stage through to delivery.

Use plain English when you can

Whether writing for the home market, for global business, as well as across generations as we've seen earlier, choose accessible, plain English. If you are a non-NE writer, don't just translate your own language into English. It can make things worse because simply translating can result in:

- over-complicated or incorrect messages;
- focusing on the specific words rather than the overall meaning;
- losing sight of the business need: for example, to write an essential call to action (what to do next).

We all need to take note that choosing unnecessarily complicated words rarely sits well in the modern workplace. For example, 'erudite' may be a 'correct' word but it's not a clever word if your readers don't understand it! Similarly, why write verbose sentences such as: 'the information we have assembled leads us to believe that…' over the more accessible: 'we find that'.

Also, don't make assumptions when you translate a word such as *actualmente* from Spanish to English that it will be the similarly sounding English word 'actually'. The correct word would be 'currently'. Don't guess at meanings, or make your readers do the same.

Regularly ask yourself:

- Will my readers recognize the words I use?
- Will they understand their meaning?
- Will these words attract and continue to engage their attention?
- Am I easily enabling the response I need?

Better to ask if you don't understand something

Problems that can arise from non-native English (non-NE) writing affect non-NE and native English readers alike. You'll see scenarios like this:

- we can't understand some or any of the non-NE writer's writing;
- we almost understand what is meant but don't ask questions as we should (either out of goodwill – or because we can't be bothered!);

- the wrong meaning then continues to be communicated, which can lead to all sorts of problems.

As an illustration, Indian English uses the expression 'trial room' which in UK or US English is 'changing room' or 'fitting room' or 'dressing room', where people try on clothes in a store before buying. In a multinational discussion forum on which expression to use, participants were really interested in this Indian English expression. Many had assumed it must mean 'courthouse', which it certainly didn't. So if you're uncertain of a meaning that might sound familiar in English but isn't what you would expect, don't be afraid to question this.

You see, you'll also find scenarios where even native US English or UK English speakers can be puzzled by different usage of an apparently common word, such as 'gas'. For both it relates to a state of matter but in US English it also means 'gasoline' – a fuel that in UK English is called 'petrol'. It's an instance, as in the previous cases I've discussed, where you may find yourself 'divided by a common language'. That's why, when in doubt, it's professional to check so you communicate effectively.

Do you work in or deal with multicultural teams? You'll find discussing what works and what doesn't will bring you all much closer together in designing effective communication.

These features can perplex readers too

The following can perplex both native English and non-NE writers alike:

Idioms, clichés and nuances

Idioms are expressions that are peculiar to a language. Simply by translating the words, non-natives may be completely unable to work out their meanings. It's true you can feel great mastering some idioms in a foreign language. I feel I am 'the bee's knees'; I am 'over the moon' about it. Do you get the drift of what I am saying, or am I pulling the wool over your eyes? Are you completely puzzled? Let me explain:

- To be 'the bee's knees' means to be really good, to be excellent.
- 'Over the moon' means delighted.
- 'To get the drift' of something means to get the general meaning.
- 'To pull the wool over someone's eyes' means to deceive them or obscure something from them.

In actual fact, native speakers may also misunderstand idioms: some are quite obscure so approach them with caution in business.

Let's consider clichés now. 'Cliché' has been imported from French into many languages, but, interestingly, it doesn't always mean the same thing in each. In German, for example, it means a stereotype, whereas in UK English it means a stale expression: something that's ineffective through overuse. A cliché often overlaps with corporate jargon or management speak and can undermine writing.

Here are some examples of clichés, with their meanings shown in brackets:

- 'In this day and age' (now).
- 'Pick the low-hanging fruit' (go for the easy option).
- 'Think outside the box' (think in an original or creative way).

'Nuance' (another word imported from French) means shade or subtlety in language. Unsurprisingly, even native writers can have difficulty understanding nuances. As an example, in one online discussion forum I noticed some English-speaking artists debating the differences between the words tint, hue, shade and so on, when describing aspects of colour. There were many suggestions but little consensus. Nuances can be tricky things.

In a business context, the subtlety in meaning between, say, 'quite proud' and 'proud' can lead to problems. You see, to a British speaker 'proud' usually has a stronger emphasis than 'quite proud'. If I tell someone I'm proud of their work, it's an absolute.

They have done very well and I'm telling them that. The moment I say that I'm 'quite proud', the perception can be that I'm diluting my pride: I am less proud than I could be. The nuance then implies that the person could have done better. That would make a material difference in a written performance review, for example.

But I once heard an American boss tell a member of staff that he was 'quite proud' of his achievements. I could hear his intonation in the spoken words. This distinctly told me that he was using 'quite proud' to mean 'very proud'. But we can't hear intonation in writing (except when we SHOUT through capital letters or through emoticons, which signify emotions). So nuances that mean different things to different people, might not make commercial sense when you think about it.

Standard and online dictionaries, and the lure of cut and paste!

Always check the meanings and spellings of words when unsure. And, whatever you do, don't feel you have to use the most complicated word your dictionary offers!

Let's say you're a non-NE writer using an online dictionary and you type a word in your own language for 'outcome'. You see a selection of English translation words. I tried this in German once and the online dictionary offered, amongst other words, corollary and consecution. Corollary is a word that people may know but it's only used in a very specific context. Consecution, though? That's very technical and rarely used in everyday business writing.

None of us should feel we must choose the most complicated 'intelligent-sounding' choice – which is often the longest – when we face a bewildering selection of words to choose from. Think before you ditch 'outcome', which almost everyone will understand, for 'consecution'!

Look for the word that people really use. Don't be disappointed if this is more prosaic than the language of Shakespeare. You write intelligently in English for business when your readers understand you.

Is there a particular example you've encountered? Why not jot it down while the subject is fresh in your mind? Consider discussing any issues with your boss and colleagues to get a fix on how to deal with them.

Muddled business writing costs on so many levels

In business we communicate by speech and writing and visuals. But we only succeed if we get our intended message across without distortion.

Here's a clear example of a distorted message:

> Identifying business writing has to be about messages. Present them you should then in a key that will engage readers' attention – and make them want way to read more.

How did you react to this piece of writing? Did you even try to make any sense of it? Did you decode it? Because that is precisely what you would have had to do.

Here's the decoded message:

> Business writing has to be about identifying key messages. You should then present them in a way that will engage readers' attention – and make them want to read more.

You can see how distortion makes a mockery of good advice – yet, sadly, you'll still find many jumbled messages in the workplace.

Let's identify differing ways readers can react to muddled messages. My findings include:

- Readers might not be bothered to work out the meaning. Unimpressed, they might walk away from the 'message' – and from the business that it belongs to.

- Readers might also tell others the bad news.

- Readers might try to work out a meaning: they might decipher it wrongly and do nothing.

- Or they might take the wrong action.
- Readers cannot understand and they need to ask for clarification.
- Readers might be offended and not tell you.
- Readers might complain to you.

Can you see the commercial implications involved in these scenarios? They are all negative, such as:

- Inaction from readers, or their failure to react the desired way.
- Lost custom and goodwill speak for themselves and affect your profits.
- A bad reputation (spread by unhappy readers telling others – especially detrimental when this goes viral as we saw in Chapter 5) can undermine your success and damage your business.
- Being on the receiving end of wrong action is clearly appalling for any business.
- Clarifying messages involves doing the same job twice or more.
- Upsetting readers is never going to be good for any business.
- Complaints may be good news in one sense (you get to hear what your customer thinks, and you can change) but they are also bad news – and they cost you.

Activity: What problems have you seen at work as a result of distorted messages? Why was that? What 'notes to self' can you jot down?

Tune in to how English continues to evolve

We're seeing how business writing is in a state of flux and the English language also continues to change. Indeed, modern English has evolved from so many influences: Anglo-Saxon, Latin, Greek,

French, Celtic, Dutch and a colonial past. The list goes on – and has furnished a fantastically rich English vocabulary.

One interesting language consideration you may notice when using English in business is an ongoing debate where on one side are those who believe in prescribing rules of traditional grammar, etc. On the other are those who believe it's more about examining how language evolves, describing new practices and adopting current usage.

Let's look at one example. Traditionalist, prescriptive English teachers might discourage writing, say, 'to boldly go', as this splits the infinitive form of the verb 'to go'. They would argue you must write 'to go boldly'. Don't be puzzled if you encounter such prescriptivism in other cases too, maybe in some 'traditional', maybe older-generation workplaces. If managers require you to write like that, you'll have to listen. But in time, they are quite likely to accept that upcoming generations' rather more conversational style of writing, with 'new rules' of grammar, is the one to follow.

Once again, tune in to what's expected by your target readership. Sometimes you'll find a middle course works best and longest – neither overly traditional nor restricted to, say, the latest expressions, which may not pass the test of time.

Non-native English writers can have an advantage!

Forward-thinking, successful companies often actively encourage and train non-NE employees to perfect the English writing skills they need. A positive learning culture such as this can foster attention to quality and professionalism. It can even result in non-NE staff making more effort than native speakers in avoiding confusion and misunderstandings.

Native English writers: beware of complacency!

Native speakers of any language can assume they are proficient in their own language, so 'of course people understand what we say and write'. But it's not necessarily true. Ideally, companies should assess writing ability when recruiting and/or promoting employees into jobs that need this skill (and, actually, which jobs don't?). Otherwise complacency sets in – and complacency drains the lifeblood of any organization. It's how companies lose the competitive edge.

Let's see some practical examples where native English writers got it wrong and paid the price.

An upmarket hotel opened its new restaurant, meant to be called The Brasserie. Unfortunately, nobody checked the correct spelling of this French word. The restaurant opened to great fanfare. The trouble was, it was called The Brassiere. It was not long before it was ridiculed in the national press – but it was long enough for it to lose face (and money on the signage, menus and advertising, all of which had to be redone).

Another unfortunate piece of writing by a native English speaker was this: 'I feel I have become a prawn in the game.' He actually meant to write 'pawn in the game' (using a chess analogy) but the extra letter made a nonsense of this.

So it's certainly not just non-native English writers who make mistakes. But the uplifting fact is that, whatever the nationality, it's virtually always the good who have the passion to strive to be better!

Your checklist for action

To use business English at work, your words and the framework that surround them have to be perfect. It's achievable, so don't set the bar lower! There are stark consequences of getting it wrong, as we keep seeing: business writing mistakes (including unclear, confusing or alienating messages) can equal lost cash, custom or goodwill.

For these reasons:

- If unable to explain things as precisely as you would like, focus on the main messages that are essential for readers to know (except for contracts, technical documents, etc, where every detail matters!).

- Make sure you get your message right for your recipient: more complicated text can be counterproductive, and confusing for all.

- If you're preoccupied with the detail of describing what you do, you can lose sight of the bigger picture (eg the need to express how you do it better than the rest, to win and retain custom).

- Do the work for your readers: make sure your messages are not losing you (or them) time or money.

- No matter how good our English language skills are, we need to get successful, professional messages across.

- Discuss any points arising from this chapter with colleagues, to flag up any general or specific concerns (especially helpful for bringing multicultural and/or multigenerational teams closer).

(more on this shortly) do the job more effectively? It's true that where every conceivable time zone may have to be covered in global business, e-mails can work best. But assess each task on its merits as poor use of e-mail creates inefficiency in the workplace. We're also losing many traditional problem-solving skills as a direct result as it's easy to pass messages on without dealing with them. Other factors need to be addressed as well. Non-native and native English writers often write over-concisely at the cost of not making complete sense. And now that an estimated 55 per cent of all e-mails are opened on mobile devices, your well-designed, helpful format may be lost.

The 'on the move' mobile device reader processes information in a different way too: another reason to avoid the beginning, middle and end writing of yesteryear. You have to write smarter than ever before, to get key messages across sooner.

Writing e-mails

When it comes to writing e-mails, two fundamental findings emerge:

- E-mails are written by virtually all levels of staff in all types of company. Largely gone are the days of the traditional secretary: we mostly have to design our writing ourselves.

- Looking at the statistics, it's easy to see how such vast e-mail usage can lead to information overload. So it's crucial to maintain quality and make things as relevant and easy as possible for the reader, so your e-mails stand out for the right reasons – not because your English or your content is wrong.

E-mail scenarios to watch out for

Sending too quickly

We all do it: we type our messages and click on the send button without checking them first. Speed of response can seem like a

08
E-mail and instant messaging

General

In e-mail and instant messaging (IM), the focus is on the one-to-one recipient or the relatively 'captive audiences' of your e-mail thread or address book contacts. It contrasts with social media's main focus on writing to interest and engage a wider (often specifically targeted) audience.

E-mail remains a predominant form of business writing today; and inestimable billions of e-mails are sent worldwide each day. This doesn't mean to say volume equates with effectiveness as a business writing medium. The problem can be that every sender feels their e-mail is the most important one, and more words (and more people copied in, sometimes almost on autopilot) not only leads to information overload but can also come over as 'talking all day about nothing'! It's no good having a big inbox with little content. No wonder some companies actually have a policy of deleting e-mails that remain unread after a certain time. Their view is if the sender hasn't followed up, maybe by phone, then the message can't have been that important! Messages need to be clear and get to the point so readers don't have to get back to you with 'What do you want from me?'

Let's look at your business. How many e-mails do you write in a week at work? Do you treat them all as professional, corporate communication? If you hesitate, the chances are that you don't – and if not, why not? Your readers and your competitors may be ahead of you on this. Also, do you check each time you use e-mail that it is the right medium? Would a phone call, face-to-face conversation, or IM must but can create particular problems for native and non-native English writers alike. Spelling and grammar mistakes, abrupt tone, overreacting or simply not answering questions can all make readers judge your e-mails in a negative light. Take the time you need to get it right.

Draft folder

If you are really pressured and know you can't send your e-mail by return, think about drafting a reply. Move it into your draft folder until you can complete it, maybe after asking someone for help.

CC or cc

This stands for 'carbon copy'. The cc field is for copying your e-mail to other recipients so they see the same message as the main addressee. Don't overuse this feature and copy in people unnecessarily, as a matter of course. It causes information overload. If you use a cc internally within your company, it's not generally a problem when those listed in the cc field see others' e-mail addresses. But where your cc field includes the e-mail addresses of external recipients, you may get into trouble because of privacy and data protection laws. Spammers can also use these lists – and forwarded e-mail addresses can harbour viruses.

BCC or bcc

This stands for 'blind carbon copy'. It means that the copy of the e-mail message is sent to a recipient whose address cannot be seen by other recipients. This is useful where confidentiality is required.

Multilingual and other e-mail threads

When it comes to business communication, there is nothing more frustrating, confusing or even downright rude than someone e-mailing you a message you literally cannot understand! Just because you are both corresponding in English, it's not suddenly going to mean that your recipient understands your language. This might seem obvious, yet the widespread use of e-mail threads can make a mockery of this need for clarity.

Read the following e-mail thread starting from bottom to top, to see how a multilingual thread can lead to confusion:

De: Paul Lederer
À: Harry Brown
Objet: Lead Project A

Hi Harry
Pierre Marceau passed me your request. We've contacted Pilar
Lopez as she's the project manager for this and you'll find her
e-mail on this below.
Kind regards
Paul

From: Pilar Lopez
To: Paul Lederer
Subject: Lead Project A

Paul,
¡Consigue que me llame!
gracias
Pilar

De: Paul Lederer
À: Pilar Lopez
Objet: Lead Project A

Pilar,
I think you're probably the best person to deal with the question posed below. Am I right? I know that as you are new to the company, you have difficulty writing in English, so feel free to reply to this in Spanish as I'll understand.
Regards,
Paul

De: Pierre Marceau
À: Paul Lederer
Objet: Lead Project A

Paul,
Je n'ai pas les informations dont Harry a besoin. Peux-tu l'aider ?
Merci
Pierre

From: Harry Brown
To: Pierre Marceau
Subject: Lead Project A

Hi Pierre,
I understand you have the full brief on this global project and I'm wondering if you could e-mail this over to me for familiarization, please.
Many thanks,
Harry

If I tell you that Harry Brown speaks only English, can you see how unhelpful this thread is going to be? First of all, who is dealing with Harry's request? It seems to be being passed from one person to another but Harry does not know that. The fact that Pilar Lopez has helpfully suggested (in Spanish) that Harry call her, is not something he is going to see from the thread. After all, it's Pierre who understands Spanish, not Harry. Also, why is Pilar suggesting that he give her a call, when he had asked Pierre for details by e-mail?

How is Harry going to feel? Annoyed? Yes. Alienated? Yes. Is the matter resolved? No. Harry will have to make further enquiries. To avoid this alienation (of which the sender is normally unaware, as it's rarely intentional) you could try these alternatives:

- be both courteous and efficient by summarizing, in English, the main facts of the message thread;

- avoid multilingual threads altogether;

- start each message afresh.

Embedding responses

Whether or not you embed responses is a question of knowing how well this method works both for you and your recipients. Younger generations often cannot imagine working any other way. For others it's actually stressful, especially for managers left to weave together perhaps five differing views, all embedded into the original e-mail.

Have you ever had to figure out what the overall picture is, at the end of a complicated trail of embedded messages? It's challenging enough in your native language! Imagine how much worse this will be where you have to try to interpret broken or variant English too. There's a point at which embedding messages can become 'hiding messages'. Quit before you get to that point – and start a new e-mail! This example shows you how tricky it can be to decipher embedded text. Let's say your e-mail asks four people in four different countries for their observations. You suggest they each embed their comments using a different colour. So Alexei in Russia chooses dark blue, Kentaro in Japan chooses teal, Cora in the Netherlands chooses red (and chooses to use capitals as well), and Carmen in Chile chooses brown.

Can you already see the problems that this course of action may present? It's going to become a very complicated procedure. I pity the originator who will have to try to draw the strands together to make sense. Surely it would be simpler to send a separate e-mail to each of the four? Incidentally, can you see why Cora's choice may lead to further complications? I know red is an auspicious colour in China and no doubt in other countries too. But in many countries, red embedded print is used to correct written mistakes or make criticisms. Readers may literally see a comment in red as a problem – even if it's actually meant to be helpful and positive.

Cora has also chosen to use capitals. According to accepted e-mail etiquette, capitals throughout an e-mail signify that you're SHOUTING. Cora's comments could then appear to be criticisms, although she may never realize this or the fact that she might be offending readers as a result. So do evaluate when and how to embed messages and when to avoid this writing technique.

Structure your e-mails

E-mail is largely viewed as a form of communication that is halfway between conversation and formal business writing. Many people feel this means they can type their ideas:

- in the English words that just occur to them;
- in no particular order;
- with no stated objectives;
- with no attention to punctuation, grammar or any other quality control;
- with no attention to layout.

Yet feedback repeatedly suggests that readers don't like reading solid blocks of text. What's more, if they don't like the look of a piece of writing, they may intuitively feel they are not going to like its content. This feeling can even go so far as to prevent them from bothering to read it.

When it comes to our personal e-mail, and the world of blogging, we can relax to an extent. These are areas where we can let our writing just capture our thoughts, more or less exactly in the English in which they spill out (though we still have to observe the constraints of the law, including libel, etc). Readers are more likely to have the time and the inclination to read our outpourings and storytelling – but this approach is definitely best avoided for business e-mail.

My tips apply even more if you are writing English for a cross-cultural audience. Use an easy-to-read font, design good layout and enter some carriage returns when you type, so that your words are not bunched up and difficult to read.

Leave some white space by using paragraphs for new topics; people will thank you for it because, by and large, people like white space. Structure every e-mail to help readers see exactly what your points are and where the e-mail is leading: that is, its purpose and who does what and when.

If you do not make the purpose, the time frame and any call to action clear, then people might not respond. And, of course, if your e-mail has no purpose, then don't write it!

Designing how you write e-mails

Here are some guidelines to help you structure your e-mails well.

Corporate communication

Is there a corporate style regarding layout? Do you have a corporate font? Is the font you use easily readable, such as Arial, Tahoma or Verdana? Is the point size you use large enough? (12 point or above is often recommended.) Don't just use lower case alone: corporate e-mail should still be in standardized English. Are you using your spellcheck and grammar check – and have you selected the correct variety of English?

Tone and appropriateness

Probably most reader complaints about e-mails relate to poor tone and inappropriate subject matter. Regarding the first point, be aware that you need to introduce the right tone for your target audience in each e-mail, as we have seen earlier.

Check whether you are using the right style of English:

- Is 'Hi' the right opening salutation?

- Or should you use 'Hello' or 'Dear' followed by the recipient's first name or title and surname?

- Or is it sufficient simply to use their first name alone, for example, 'Paolo'? (Many find this approach curt.)

Most companies I work with do use 'Hi' as the default salutation but this is not a 'one size fits all' solution as there are people who don't like it. When in doubt, using mirroring techniques can be useful in cross-cultural situations. By this I mean that, where feasible, you try replying to readers in a similar way to the way they address you.

Always remember that if you are not prepared to say a particular thing face to face, or if you would not be happy for other people to see your e-mail (including people you may not know about), then do not write it!

Use a good subject heading; refresh it regularly

If you want people to open your e-mail, write an interesting headline. If it's compelling, so much the better! For instance, I once received an e-mail from a company that I'd heard of but didn't actually know. Their subject heading was: 'Awards & important social media updates'. I opened it. Why? Do you think it was to see what awards they had won? No, it wasn't. The interest for me was to check on the 'important' social media updates. But good for them, they got the reputational message across that they had won awards!

Always think of meaningful subject headings for your readers. 'Update on Project A at end of week 30' is going to be a better heading than simply 'Project A'. In subsequent e-mails refresh the headings, so messages always reflect the current picture wherever possible. How helpful is that heading about week 30 when you're actually discussing progress at week 40?

Regularly refresh e-mails

I've discussed problems that can arise from multilingual e-mail threads. Let me just reinforce the message now: try to get into the habit of stopping e-mail threads, maybe after the third message. Start a new e-mail and if you need to carry information over, just recap the key points.

Before you send

- Re-read your e-mail and check that your communication in English is correct on every level.
- Make sure it doesn't include previous e-mail threads that may not be appropriate to forward on to the new reader(s).
- Have you included any attachments? Are they in English too?
- If you have copied somebody in, have you explained why?
- Is the subject heading good?
- Is the e-mail easy to read (font style and size, etc)?

After sending

Check after the event (a day, two days, a week?) that you have achieved the outcome you want. Check that the English you have written has worked for your needs.

Instant messaging and texting

Instant messaging (IM) and text messaging (SMS) are some of the fastest-growing areas of business communication and are widely used in social media too via services such as WhatsApp, Viber, etc.

Both are predominantly text based but instant messaging is more about real-time, quick-fire replies between two or more correspondents (usually internally within a business though you can invite external members for specific projects). Unlike e-mail, you can set settings, to see who is on- or offline, or busy – and alert them to contact you at a mutually convenient time if necessary.

It's a really useful medium where:

- things need to be moved quickly along (for example, sales or financial teams needing the latest figures, or people needing to know quickly about a bump in negotiations);
- teams and communities need to be kept in the loop and can dip in and out of the ongoing newsfeed;
- you need group chat or a conference;
- those in the group have implicitly given members permission to the effect 'if you haven't heard from me on e-mail or phone, contact me in real time on WhatsApp' (or alternative).

It's also noticeable how employees, especially upcoming generations, can be more comfortable with IM over voice chat in these situations and this is another reason for its effectiveness in business writing.

That said, we've seen the problems in sending e-mails too quickly, so it's easy to see how the rapid reply feature of messaging builds in more hazards to avoid! Around the world, we see something very noticeable in business communication generally as a result. Just take a look at any you have received recently. Even if you work in a highly traditional organization, I bet you'll see abbreviated language, emoticons, and imprecise spellings, grammar and punctuation.

Socially, it's what we expect in this medium, poised as it is some-where between e-mail and conversation. But it's best to think this through in your workplace. Do you want the increasingly casual style of instant messaging where it's quite normal to express emotions, in words or via emoticons or even via use of punctuation, to cross over into your standard business e-mails too?

It's a good point to discuss with colleagues because we're seeing the business e-mail style (see Example 1) often change to very or slightly casual textspeak (see Examples 2 and 3):

Example 1

John: Hi. Please may we have a meeting tomorrow?

Jane: Yes, certainly. Shall we say 9.30 am? I look forward to catching up with you.

Example 2

John: U cool with mtg tom?

Jane: Heyyyy no worries CU tom. 9.30. Catch up then lol

Example 3

Josh: Hey, are you around tomorrow for a quick meeting?

Emily: Yeah sure – 9:30 ok?

Josh: Perfect!

Emily: Cool – catch up then! ☺

Example 1 shows a fairly traditional style; Example 2 the style that we saw some years ago, which already looks very old-fashioned; and Example 3 shows what we often see today. But even that will date. 'Cool' already isn't a word that Gen Z and other upcoming generations are likely to use.

Interestingly, the fairly traditional conversational style in Example 1 is likely to keep the best currency across the ever-changing generations in the workplace and across diverse cultures. Once again, writers beware the possible pitfalls to avoid! Everyone needs to understand your writing and not feel alienated by modern-day slang or colloquialisms that (even unintentionally) can have the undesired effect of putting up barriers: 'you're not in my zone' – or that become dated without you realizing! Inclusive language works best in today's and tomorrow's workplace.

A really useful exercise would be for you to have inter-generational discussions in the workplace on this topic. Not enough companies do.

Have you also noticed how punctuation is changing in much of today's IM? Although language always changes, many observe that since the internet arrived, it has never changed so fast.

For this reason, I can't go into all the variations in punctuation we now see creeping into our casual business communication. Best you keep up to speed with what you see happening around you. But I'll outline some common variations we're seeing.

Punctuation marks in IM can signify more than grammar features: they can signify emotions too. For instance, now that hitting *enter* shows when our instant message (or social media post) ends, the period or full stop can be viewed as redundant. Many think that inserting it signifies 'discussion ended' – which is harsh, even angry.

An ellipsis, usually appearing as three dots in a sentence or phrase, is another punctuation mark now used creatively in IM. Originally, an ellipsis indicated that something had been left out of the writing intentionally, that did not affect the overall meaning, eg: 'the government doesn't intend to change the law…it's for the next administration to do this.' The writer didn't feel it necessary to explain (presumably again) which law they were referring to. Alternatively, an ellipsis could suggest a pause, eg 'That's a great idea…we'll implement it next week.'

But what we can now see in IM – and overspilling into other business writing – is an ellipsis used to signify:

- conversational 'hmms' or 'erms' to soften the text;
- indicators of 'food for thought' for writer and/or reader alike (eg 'let's see...might work) which don't necessarily lead to action;
- less positive meanings such as impatience or dissent (eg This will work?... where the ellipsis implies: 'no it won't!').

So because of the variety of interpretations, I suggest you think carefully, as business writing needs to be crystal clear.

On this theme of overspilling of styles, in Chapter 5 we looked at examples of how instant messaging interaction with customers via social media (regarding complaints, for example) is leading to readers expecting a more conversational style in corporate communication generally.

The pressing need now is how to define its use within your organization. You need to check what is acceptable.

As a first step, understanding the scenarios when texting or instant messaging is going to help your business productivity. Is it something that's essential to update people on crisis management, project status, orders, complaints, journey delays, meetings and other time-sensitive matters where deadlines are critical? If you have a few seconds free that can be a most effective use of time – and we've also seen in Chapter 5 how speed of response matters when dealing with customers via instant messaging on social media.

On a very practical level, just as you need to think about your readers' proficiency in English in other writing tasks, don't forget this applies equally in the fast-moving messaging arena. Just because you may be able to fire off, let's say, five points – if not simultaneously, at least in quick succession – doesn't mean your correspondent can reply as speedily.

Have you personally ever seen the 'wrong answers' coming in from your respondent – in the sense that they don't align sequentially with your questions? Do you always wait for an answer to come in when you see the legend '*(name) is typing*' before typing your next question? Many don't! Then, far from messaging providing the solution, it creates the problem! It's just as important to write effectively in texts and IM as in any other form of writing. Try one question at a time and allow adequate time for the reply you need to arrive.

Instant messaging and texting can also create the same sorts of barriers as other jargon does. LOL is frequently used and can be taken to mean both 'laugh out loud' or 'lots of love'. Can you see the problems when abbreviations can perhaps unintentionally embarrass people into having to admit they actively don't like it or find it inappropriate? They can be equally embarrassed by not understanding it – or having to pretend that they do. So tread with care.

Here are some tips to help:

- Consider a business user policy that's separate from your personal use and which can include status/availability settings (within the system application you use), and whether you use texting and messaging for internal and external use.

- As part of this policy, consider whether sensitive or negative information can or should ever be relayed by this method rather than face to face or by formal notification.

- Remember that all written messages can provide an audit trail. Be professional: project company values and quality – and maintain reputation (yours and others').

- Work out which expressions have common currency so readers understand any shorthand you use.

- If you do use emoticons and emojis (small digital icons that signify feelings) only use those that are right for your reader. For example, the 'thumbs up' sign expresses positivity to some cultures but is offensive to others. Also be aware that not all devices will display the emoticons yours does.

- Keep texting and messaging only for quick response, not for the detail.

- As with e-mail, don't let speed trap you into inferior writing. Abbreviated spelling may be acceptable but each message has to be both organized and understood.

- Observe etiquette: just because you are free for those seconds, you might be interrupting someone else's meeting, etc, even if their status setting indicates they are available. Ask when they can reply if you don't hear by return.

- Etiquette also involves the right tone – and understanding recipients' preferred style.

- As with e-mail, let readers know where the message is leading and what response you need.

- It may be better to deal with one message at a time because of the 'on the go' nature of the medium. Use line breaks to avoid run-on sentences that are difficult to decipher.

- Check whether texting or messaging mode is migrating into your other business communication and what guidelines you may need to have in place to uphold quality and values.

> **Activity:** Discuss the best use of texting and instant messaging with colleagues and how this may impact on your other corporate communication. Collaborate on the code you will use to avoid misunderstandings, even offence. It's also helpful to decide on the salutations/endings you will use (as required). You might be surprised how important this is in workplaces to avoid irritated readers' faces!

Your checklist for action

Before you press send, ask yourself:

- Is e-mail or instant messaging the right communication medium? Is your English fit for purpose? E-writing is corporate communication and your English has to be professional.

- Have you made the e-mail subject heading relevant so people want to/know they must read it?

- In exchanges, have you refreshed your headings (if appropriate) and updated details that have changed?

- Did you get to the point in accessible language so readers know where you are leading?

- Did you systematically read and cover the points in the e-mail or message to which you are replying?

- Is embedding responses appropriate for your community or does it generate confusion?

- Have you done a spellcheck and grammar check on your e-mails, using the correct variety of English?

- Have you overreacted? If you are not prepared to say your message face to face or let it be seen by others, you should not send it.

- If you can see that someone is typing a response, do you wait for it to arrive before firing off another instant message in the conversation?

- Would it be a problem for you or your organization if this e-mail or message is forwarded in its entirety to other people without your knowledge? Don't forget that all written messages can be used in an audit trail.

- Are you sending the attachments you promised?

- If you are copying someone in, have you explained why?

- Have you developed the right rapport with your readers and met their business and cultural expectations?

- Have you set (and are you remembering to update) your IM status?

- Check whether messaging mode is migrating into your other more formal business communication and what guidelines you may need to have in place to uphold quality and values.

- Are you keeping up to date on changing language and punctuation in business writing today?

09
Punctuation and grammar tips

Why punctuation and grammar matter

This extract shows what unpunctuated writing looks like:

> mr jones the companys hr director called mrs smith into his
> office for an update on the latest recruitment drive he wanted
> to know whether the online application system was working
> reports had filtered through that all was not going to plan mrs
> smith explained that candidates were certainly experiencing
> problems as the systems had crashed in her opinion it would
> be better to extend the closing date would he be prepared to
> authorize this

Did you have any problem deciphering this? A lot of people will
find it difficult. If we write poetry we may actively want people to
work out the meaning. We may even want them to create their own
meaning; but this should not apply to business writing!

In writing, punctuation is an aid that helps our readers to understand our messages. The extract could be punctuated a number of
ways. I will use one way to show how it becomes easier to read:

> Mr Jones, the company's HR director, called Mrs Smith into
> his office for an update on the latest recruitment drive. He
> wanted to know whether the online application system was
> working. Reports had filtered through that all was not going to
> plan.

Mrs Smith explained that candidates were certainly experiencing problems as the systems had crashed. In her opinion, it would be better to extend the closing date.

Would he be prepared to authorize this?

You see, punctuation and grammar are aids that help writing to be understood and help us to communicate clearly. If like most people you find some aspects challenging, it can be a good idea to ask a line manager or a mentor if you're unsure. Ideally, managers should be encouraged to offer active support to people with dyslexia or other writing challenges too. Top entrepreneur Richard Branson is dyslexic yet writes best-selling business books and much-admired blogs, as we've seen. He says he relies on his right-hand people to check his English before he publishes because he knows that this matters. That's an inspirational message. The best leaders encourage supportive teamwork so that companies get things right on all levels.

So, all the topics in this chapter are an essential component in the word power skills writing system. When you have a good grasp of the principles, you will feel secure in the knowledge that your sentences will work because you have *designed* them to work. And if you're not sure about something, you will have the confidence to ask for help.

Punctuation and other marks

English terms and symbols used to describe punctuation marks are:

Capital letters or upper case: A, B, C

Lower case: a, b, c

Comma: ,

Full stop (UK English) or period (UK and US English) or dot: .

Speech or double quotation marks or inverted commas: " "

Speech or single quotation marks or inverted commas: ' '

Question mark: ?

Exclamation mark: !

Apostrophe: '

Hyphen or dash: -

Slash or stroke: /

Brackets: ( )

Square brackets: [ ]

Ampersand: &

'At' sign: @

Colon: :

Semicolon: ;

Asterisk: *

Parts of speech and other grammar

Parts of speech

In English grammar, words are categorized into what we term parts of speech. These include nouns, pronouns, adjectives, verbs, adverbs, prepositions, conjunctions and interjections.

A noun names a person, place or thing. For example:

girl, London, newspaper;

The man drank his coffee.

A pronoun is a word that can take the place of a noun, and functions like it. For example:

I, this, who, he, they;

There's Peter, who won the lottery.

Notice how the noun 'Peter' became the pronoun 'who' within the same sentence.

Tune in to the changing use of pronouns in business today. My publishers offer guidelines as follows. Avoid using masculine pronouns for neutral nouns. Use 'they' and 'their' rather than 'he', 'him', 'his'.

In this way, you will find an example such as this: 'Not sure what to do? Ask your manager for their advice.' Even though 'manager' is a singular noun, the neutral plural 'their' is common usage now, in this context.

Beyond this, more pronouns are being added to the mix of English pronouns found in traditional grammar books of yesteryear. For example, some people may indicate personal, gender-fluid pronouns they want you to use when addressing them, such as 'ze' or 'hir' as their preferred third-person singular pronouns over 'he' or 'she', etc.

There are many other variations that this book hasn't the scope to include, and besides it is very much about individuals' personal preferences, so please do take the time to research your readers and mirror to them what they expect. It's very much about tailoring your writing and tuning in to the ongoing changes. It's essential to do this to communicate effectively and respectfully with your target audience.

An adjective is a word that describes a noun. For example:

red, lovely, clever;

That is a lovely photo.

A verb is a 'doing word' or describes a state of being. For example:

write, run, work, be;

She is an assistant who works hard.

Sometimes a verb needs two or three words to complete it. For example:

I am working in Moscow this week.

You will be travelling first class.

An adverb is a word that describes a verb. For example:

fast, happily, later, urgently;

The project manager always delivered on time.

In that last example there is an adverb, 'always', and an adverbial phrase, 'on time', which describe the verb 'delivered'.

A preposition is a word that links a noun to another noun. For example:

to, on, under, in;

Please put the papers on the desk.

A conjunction is a word that joins words or sentences. For example:

and, but, or, so;

I need a flipchart but that is all.

An interjection is a short exclamation, often followed by an exclamation mark (!). For example:

hi! oh!

Some other grammatical points of interest

Commas can separate one group of words in a sentence from another so that the meaning is clear. You will see how they flag up different meanings in these two sentences:

Sanjay, our vice-president has left the company.

Sanjay, our vice-president, has left the company.

In the first sentence, the writer is telling Sanjay that their vice-president (somebody else) has left the company. In the second sentence, the writer is telling somebody (whose name is unknown to us) that Sanjay (who is the vice-president) has left the company.

In order to use commas correctly, it helps to know that a comma signifies a brief pause. Very often, people wrongly use a comma to do the work of a full stop (period). For example:

I examined the computer, it had obviously been damaged.

As there are two complete statements here, not just a pause, we could try a full stop: 'I examined the computer. It had obviously been damaged.' However, this sounds rather stilted and a native English writer is likely to use a conjunction to add fluidity. For example: 'I examined the computer and found it had obviously been damaged.'

A comma is also used to link lists of items, groups of words, adjectives, actions and adverbs. For example:

She listed, there and then, the things she would need for her presentation: a laptop, a projector, screen, flipchart and marker pens.

Apostrophes show where one or more letters have been left out of a word. For example:

I'm = contraction of 'I am';

It's = contraction of 'it is' or 'it has';

You'll = contraction of 'you will'.

Apostrophes can also show possession or ownership. For example:

The student's rights = the rights of one student;

The students' rights = the rights of students.

The general rule is:

apostrophe before the s ('s) = singular possession;

apostrophe after the s (s') = plural possession.

Unfortunately, English always has some irregular forms, such as:

men = plural of man; but the possessive is men's;

children = plural of child; but the possessive is children's;

its = possessive of it – yet takes no apostrophe at all!

Forming plurals of nouns

As you will know, most nouns have a singular form (to denote one) and a plural (to denote more than one). There are exceptions, such as training and information. The standard way of forming plurals from singular nouns is to add 's'. But this doesn't always work, as in the case of 'child, children', 'lady, ladies', 'foot, feet', to mention a few. So do refer to mainstream English grammar advice if you need more help with this.

There is one point that I would like to address here, as it arises so often, amongst all writers. It concerns the wrong use of an apostrophe followed by 's' to signify a plural meaning. For example, 'tomato's' and 'company's'. The correct plurals are 'tomatoes' and 'companies'.

> **Activity:** Do you or your colleagues find any aspects of punctuation and grammar a challenge? It's well worth jotting down any points you feel you could work on individually, or as teams.

Vowels and consonants

In written English, 'a, e, i, o, u' are the standard vowels. The remaining letters in the alphabet are consonants.

The definite and indefinite article

The word 'the' is called the definite article and has the same form in singular and plural. The words 'a' and 'an' are known as the indefinite article and only exist in the singular. For the plural, English uses the word 'some'.

Non-native English writers can be confused about when to use the definite or indefinite article. A general guideline to help is this: when you're referring to something in general, use 'a' before a word beginning with a consonant or 'an' before a word beginning with a vowel. (Once again though, true to form, English has exceptions: some native speakers would say 'an hotel'.)

Here is an example of 'a' in this usage:

Cheese for sale: six euros a kilo, *not* 'six euros the kilo', as many non-NE writers would expect.

As an interesting aside, note that in English, goods are described as being 'for sale'. Some cultures express it the reverse way: 'to buy'. English speakers would say and write 'House for sale', not 'House to buy'. That said, I've noticed some house signs recently with the legend 'Buy *me*' – using personification as a marketing tool.

Now let's say a company receives this e-mail: 'Please can you let me know how long an order will take to deliver?' The company will consider the question as tentative – and thus non-specific. There is no order, only a general enquiry about how long it would take if somebody did place an order. Now let's say the company receives this enquiry: 'Please can you tell me how long the order will take to deliver?' The word 'the' makes this enquiry far more specific. The question is more likely to relate to an order that has been placed.

Paragraphs

Paragraphs help your reader understand the organization of your writing because each paragraph is a group of sentences about a topic. Your key messages become easy to identify and the format makes it easy for you to develop them. Paragraph headings (and sub-headings so often used on the web) are increasingly used to signpost messages and highlight structure for readers' ease.

Brackets, bullet points and dashes

Use these to break up text (especially if it's rather lengthy) so your reader is not overwhelmed, and you can also use commas, as I am doing here, to make a longish sentence more manageable. On the reverse side, too many short sentences can seem abrupt. So keep your writing interesting by mixing and matching these features, to vary and enhance your style.

Verbs and tenses

You are likely to have been taught the finer points of English grammar at school, in college or by self-study. Entire books are written on this extensive subject and it's beyond the scope of this handbook to go into any great detail. But here's an outline as a refresher. As you saw, a verb is a 'doing' word. It can consist of one or more words. The infinitive of a verb is the base form, for example 'to work', 'to give', 'to do'.

The present participle is formed by adding '-ing' to the infinitive. The 'to' part is dropped. This construction is then used with the verb 'to be' to form what are known as continuous tenses. For example: 'They are working.'

If the infinitive ends in 'e' ('to give', 'to come') the general rule is to drop the 'e' when adding the '-ing'. For example: 'He is giving', 'They are coming'.

The past participle is normally formed by adding '-ed' to the infinitive. Again, the 'to' part is dropped. This construction is used with the verb 'to have' to form perfect (completed past) tenses. For example: 'The train has departed', 'The post has arrived'.

Irregular verbs form the perfect differently, so do refer to grammar sources if you're unsure. Examples are: 'It has grown' (not grow-ed), 'The time has flown by' (not fly-ed).

Tenses

The simple tenses in English are the starting point for global business writing today.

The present tense has the same form as the infinitive (except the verb 'to be'). When the subject is 'he', 'she', 'it' or a noun, English adds '-s' or '-es'.

To form the future tense, English adds 'will' (or 'shall' – though this is less frequently used now).

To form the past tense, '-ed' is normally added to the infinitive. (Once more though, a word of caution: there are many irregular verbs where this doesn't work!) A regular example is:

Verb: to work (regular verb) simple present tense:

- o I work
- o you (singular and plural) work
- o he, she, it works
- o we work
- o they work

simple future tense:

- o I, you (singular and plural), he, she, it, we, they will work

simple past tense:

- o I, you (singular and plural), he, she, it, we, they worked

There are naturally many more tenses that you will need to study in depth and dedicated grammar resources will help you. That said, there is one tense that seems to present a real workplace problem that businesses often ask me about. It is the present continuous tense.

This is formed by using the present tense of 'to be' with the present participle of the verb in question. Let's say I want the present continuous tense of 'to write'. The forms are:

I am writing

you (singular and plural) are writing

he, she is writing

we are writing

they are writing

The question I'm so often asked is: when do we use the present continuous rather than the present tense? The answer is in three parts:

- When the action is taking place now ('I am writing this sentence at this very moment.').

- When the action is taking place now but also is carrying on into the future ('I am writing this book at this very moment – but also over the coming months.').

- When the action is planned for the future ('I am writing another book next year.').

With regard to this last sentence, the future tense would also be correct, namely: 'I will write another book next year.'

We use the present tense for more general actions or states that have no particular time reference. For example:

We drink water to survive.

If I find a mistake, I correct it.

Non-native English writers can be confused about when to write, for example:

She lives in Tokyo.

She is living in Tokyo.

Both are correct – but the second version often implies to a native English speaker that 'She is living in Tokyo (at the moment).'

Agreement of subject and verb

When a subject in a sentence is in the singular, then the verb must be in the singular too. When the subject is plural, then the verb is in the plural, in agreement with it. This is also called concord – which can trip all writers up on occasion. Examples are:

Paul is at university and so is his brother.

Paul is at university and so are his brother and sister.

They understand the reason why they have to do this.

She understands the reasons why she has to do this and why you have to do it too.

These conditions apply now. This condition applies now.

A typical error a non-native English writer may make is:

Sara has received our e-mail. Has you received it too?

Correct version:

Sara has received our e-mail. Have you received it too?

As a rule of thumb, simply work out who is doing the action and make your verb relate to who or what is doing it. In some sentences you may have to refer back to check.

Incidentally, there are certain words in English where it is possible to use a singular word in a plural sense too. Examples are: government, council, committee, company.

So in UK English, you can write:

The government is changing the law on this.

The government are changing the law on this.

The reasoning behind this is that these nouns can be viewed as entities by themselves or as bodies of people. On this track, another often-used word comes to mind. This is the word 'staff', where it means personnel. It is used as a singular in US English but exists only in the plural in UK English. So UK English says: 'The staff are taking a vote on this.' US English says: 'The staff is taking a vote on this.'

Question tags

These are used a lot in English conversation, and non-NE speakers can find them quite hard to master. As they are increasingly used in workplace writing too, here are some tips.

Speakers and writers use question tags to encourage their listeners or readers to respond. It helps check that people agree or understand what you are saying or writing.

Examples are:

It's a good outcome, isn't it?

You don't have a meeting today, do you? You can make it in time, can't you?

Examples of incorrect usage would be:

You have got the right files, isn't it?

He is wrong, doesn't he?

These kind of things are dealt with in your department, isn't it?

Correct versions of these would be:

You have got the right files, haven't you?

He is wrong, isn't he?

These kinds of things are dealt with in your department, aren't they?

Tips to help you:

- Try balancing the same verb (including whether it is singular or plural) on either side of the sentence.

- Then use a negative in the end questioning part of the sentence.

Open and closed questions

When you write English across cultures, do be aware that closed questions typically lead to a yes/no/factual answer.

Examples are:

Please can you complete this report by month end?

Is the presentation ready?

If you are dealing with a reserved culture, it could be a better idea to use an open question, such as:

Please could you give an indication of when you can complete this?

What do you think?

The recipient then has to give a fuller and more informative answer.

Comparison

Comparison of adjectives

In English, adjectives can have three degrees: positive, comparative and superlative.

The positive is just the usual form of the adjective; for example: a happy child, a large book, a comfortable chair.

The comparative is used in comparing one thing or group with another; for example: the shorter of the two brothers; ponies are smaller than horses. If it is a short word, we normally form the comparative by adding '-er'.

The superlative is used when comparing one thing or group with more than one other; for example: she is the oldest of the three sisters; that is the greatest suggestion yet. If it's a short word, we normally add '-est' to the positive.

Adjectives of three syllables or more and most adjectives of two syllables form their comparative by placing the word 'more' before the adjective. They form the superlative by placing 'most' in front of the adjective.

Some adjectives have quite different words for the comparative or superlative. For example:

good, better, best;

many, more, most;

little, less, least.

A common mistake is where writers use the superlative where they should be using the comparative. For example: 'That is the best of the two offers' is, strictly speaking, wrong. It should be: 'That is the better of the two offers.' There would have to be three or more offers for 'best' to be correct. Similarly, instead of 'She is the youngest of the two employees', the correct version would be 'She is the younger of the two employees'.

Comparison of adverbs

Short adverbs are compared in the same way as adjectives:

soon, sooner, soonest;

fast, faster, fastest.

With adverbs of two syllables or longer, you usually form the comparative and superlative by adding 'more' and 'most' to the positive degree of the word:

carefully, more carefully, most carefully;

easily, more easily, most easily.

Once again, English often comes up with irregular forms:

badly, worse, worst

well, better, best.

Fluidity in writing

Fluidity when writing English for business pays great dividends: you provide the links so that the reader does not have to work them out. This next example illustrates how.

> ABC Ltd is a well-established manufacturing company founded in 2008 that has decided to go for growth in its next five-year plan.
>
> **Despite** a downturn in the manufacturing sector generally, ABC has identified two principal ways of maintaining a successful business.
>
> **First**, management has changed the structure of the business by splitting its commercial department into two entities: sales and production.

Second, it has introduced a new outcome-based approach to assessment, which involves staff to a greater degree than before.

As a result, the company has significantly improved profits **as well as** winning a prestigious customer service award.

Your checklist for action

- Present facts clearly and present a well-argued, well-supported business case.

- Write so that readers don't have to make an effort to understand you or come back to you for further information, or wait for you to make things clear.

- Write so that readers are more likely to take a favourable view of you.

- Punctuation serves the useful purpose of helping readers read messages; and it highlights where the emphasis needs to go.

- Grammar helps you set out business writing into logical, manageable sections that help readers understand your meaning.

- Identify areas of punctuation and grammar to work on; do ask for support, if needed.

- Keep up to date on changing usage of punctuation and grammar (such as emerging pronouns), so that you continuously manage to communicate effectively and respectfully for your target readership.

- Fluidity helps you set out the points in a coherent way. All the points you make add up. Two and two must be seen to make four in your writing, not just in your sums.

10
Practical conventions and common confusions

This chapter acts as a guideline for conventions and common confusions to watch out for. Check what's relevant for you. Then join forces with colleagues to look out for these – and consider keeping a list of other things that you know regularly confuse.

Writing a date

Differing conventions

There are a number of correct ways of writing dates in English. The UK English format (which most of Europe uses) is:

DD/MM/YY, where D = day, M = month, Y = year.

This contrasts with the US format, which is:

MM/DD/YY.

And both are in contrast with the format used in Japan, for example, which is:

YY/MM/DD.

Not understanding the different conventions can create immense problems. If you have to book international transport or hotel accommodation, or arrange deliveries, meetings and so on, you'll know how important it is to input the correct dates. It can simply be a question of house style regarding the format you choose to be your default convention. But you may need to be flexible and understand that customers may be using a different convention. Check if there's any uncertainty. Sometimes be prepared to mirror their convention, as long as it's an acceptable version that makes sense. Being in business should be about embracing customers' needs, not about seeing them as 'awkward' if they do something differently.

Examples that are all perfectly acceptable in UK English are:

21 January 2025;

21st January, 2025;

21 Jan 2025;

21st Jan 2025;

21/01/25.

As I mentioned, US English uses a month/day/year format, as do some other countries. In this case, you would write:

January 21 2025;

01/21/25.

This particular date isn't too problematic because we know that there are not 21 months in a year. But where readers don't understand the differences between the UK and US conventions, they could have problems with a date such as 03/06/25. In the UK this denotes 3 June 2025, but in the United States it denotes 6 March 2025.

International date format

This was devised to make the way we write dates internationally understandable. It is based on the following format:

YYYY – MM – DD.

In this format, YYYY refers to all the digits (eg 2025), MM refers to the month (01 to 12) and DD refers to the day (01 to 31).

When there is any doubt, it's really useful to write your dates in English this way.

Some confusions

Days and weeks

If you write 'next Tuesday', people can get confused as to whether you're referring to the first Tuesday that follows after the day you wrote this – or whether you mean a Tuesday in another week. So, as an example, if you write it on a Monday, is 'next Tuesday' the following day (which I would take it to mean), or the Tuesday of the following week? If you write it on a Friday, it is easier to see that it would have to be the Tuesday of the following week.

'This coming Tuesday' has the same meaning as 'next Tuesday'. So do be careful. I know of instances where misunderstandings about this have led to missed appointments. Ironically, the people who misunderstand the correct use of the expression are the ones who can get angry. Also, imagine the cost if you book foreign travel for the wrong date. The best arrangement is always to write the precise date you mean, for example: 'next Tuesday, 4th November'.

'In a couple of weeks' literally means 'in two weeks', as 'couple' means 'two' in English. It is true that 'a couple of weeks' can be used in a looser sense, meaning in about two weeks, but it's best to check. As another example, the Dutch expression *'paar dagen'* means a few days, but the Dutch often wrongly translate this into English as 'a couple', or 'two' days. So where orders are concerned, it's always best to clarify what is meant.

'Next Monday week' means 'a week from next Monday'. 'Over a week' in English means 'in more than a week's time'. But non-NE writers often use the expression 'over a week' to mean in a week's time, that is, one week from now. An example would be: 'The delivery will be over a week.' Again be careful if you are dealing with orders, because you can confuse.

'A fortnight' means two weeks. I find that many nationalities are unaware of this word, so it can be better to avoid it.

Time off

In UK English, people usually refer to their 'holidays', where US English uses 'vacation'. Time off work for holidays is referred to as 'leave'; time off through illness is 'sick leave'.

Public and bank holidays

A public holiday is an official holiday for the majority of a state or country. In the UK, the term 'bank holiday' is used when the public holiday falls on a weekday when banks are closed by law. When you write about public holidays or bank holidays globally, be aware that they can vary from country to country, usually being cultural in origin.

Time

Things can go seriously wrong when different nationalities fail to understand that they may have differing conventions for writing times. People fail to turn up to meetings at the right time, they miss flights, deadlines: in short, if a matter is time bound it can go wrong. And what in business is not linked to time? Here are some guidelines to help.

UK English

All these written versions are correct in English:

The meeting starts at 09.00.

The meeting starts at 9am (or 9 am or 9 a.m.).

The meeting starts at nine o'clock in the morning.

The meeting starts at nine in the morning.

English usage includes both the 12-hour clock (morning and afternoon) and the 24-hour clock (especially for timetables), so:

09.00 means nine o'clock in the morning;

21.00 means nine o'clock in the evening.

Strangely enough, 24.00 is also 0.00 hours!

If we write in English, 'The meeting starts at half past eight', this could mean 'The meeting starts at 08.30' or 'The meeting starts at 20.30'.

Often, we'll know from context which is correct. For example, if meetings are held during normal office hours, then half past eight in the morning is the more likely time. But say we work in a staggered-hours environment, then it could be a morning or an evening meeting. You need to clarify.

Differing conventions in different countries

Mishaps or missed meetings and other appointments all arise when we fail to realize that the way different countries express time isn't standard. For example, the United States does not generally use the 24-hour clock (except specifically by some professions: for example, the military, the police, the medical profession). Some countries (eg Germany) use a format to express half an hour before an hour. This is alien to native English writing – where half past six, for example, should be expressed as 'half seven' to the German way of thinking.

Don't underestimate how problematic failing to appreciate this source of misunderstanding can be. Do ensure that everyone understands how to write and read times in English, for the sake of efficiency.

Numbers

If you are writing numbers in English, also be aware that different nationalities may interpret the numbers differently. Look how your order books – and your bottom line – could be affected. For example, the words 'billion' and 'trillion' can have completely different meanings in the UK, Germany, France and the United States. But a zillion means a large indeterminate number, so that expression at least is standard!

A fairly old imperial expression you will still find on occasion is dozen. It means 12.

You use a comma when you write a number comprising four or more digits. Counting from right to left, you place the comma after each three digits:

1,000;

10,000;

100,000;

100,000,000.

How the decimal point is written in English

'Decimal point' is the UK English term for the dot placed after the figure that represents units in a decimal fraction: for example, 9.6. This may differ from the way you express the decimal point in your language. You may be used to using a comma – for example 9,6 – or you may express 100,000,000 as 100.000.000. It's not overly confusing but it's best to be aware of this difference when you write in English.

Decimal points when writing monetary units in English

Some nationalities express their decimal currencies using commas where there is a decimal fraction: €1,80. If you are writing a tariff in English, you express this amount as: €1.80

Other punctuation differences are apparent in the following written representation of the same number. The UK English version is the first of these:

890,123.50

890.123,50

Measurements

Do you have to write measurements in English? If you're writing globally, do be aware that different countries use different systems. Broadly speaking, these are called metric and imperial.

The United States largely uses imperial and the UK and other countries may use a combination. You will need to research if you're involved in orders that use either system. To give you an idea, some differences are as follows:

Metric system:

o length: centimetre, metre, kilometre (US spelling: meter, etc);

o weight: gram, kilogram, tonne;

o capacity: millilitre (ml), litre (US spelling liter, etc);

o temperature: centigrade or Celsius.

Imperial system:

o length: inch, foot, yard, mile;

o weight: ounce, pound, ton;

o capacity: fluid ounce, pint, gallon;

o temperature: Fahrenheit.

Even within the imperial system, you'll find that a US ton is not the same as a UK ton, and a US gallon is different to a UK gallon.

Temperatures are also written using different systems:

centigrade or Celsius: freezing point of pure water 0° (degrees); boiling point 100°;

Fahrenheit: freezing point of pure water 32°; boiling point 212°.

Words that can confuse both native English and non-native English writers

Some words repeatedly cause businesses confusion. Sometimes it's because different people within the same company set their computer spellcheck to different varieties of English. Often homonyms confuse. These are words that have the same sound but can have different meanings and spellings.

Words or spellings that commonly confuse

Here are some commonly confused words, together with examples of correct usage.

Receive and recieve

The correct version is 'receive'. A useful rule in English spelling is that after the letter 'c' the letter 'e' goes before 'i'.

Stationary and stationery

'Stationary' means standing still: for example, 'The careless driver crashed into a stationary car.'

'Stationery' means writing and printing materials: for example, 'I have ordered new business stationery for my office.'

Licence and license, practice and practise

In UK English, the nouns relating to these words end in 'ce'. The verbs end in 'se'. For example:

Which doctor's practice do you go to? (Practice = noun: the doctor's place of work.)

You should practise what you preach. (Practise = verb.)

In US English it's completely different. 'Practice' (note the *c*) and 'license' (note the *s*) are always the spellings, no matter whether they are nouns or verbs. For example:

He has a valid license (noun), so he is licensed (verb) to drive here.

The best practice (noun) is to practice (verb) what you preach.

Compliment and complement

'Compliment' is a noun or verb meaning praising or admiring. 'Complement' is a noun or verb meaning a thing that completes something else. For example:

We are always delighted to receive a compliment from a customer.

When dining, the right ambience complements the meal.

Loose and lose

'Loose' is an adjective that means not tightly packed or fixed. For example:

There is a loose connection in the wiring system.

'Lose' is a verb that means cease to have, be unable to find. For example:

If we lose their parcel we will also lose their custom.

There and their

'There' is an adverb meaning in that place. 'Their' is an adjective meaning belonging to them. For example:

The file you need is over there. It will be their turn next.

Where, were and we're

'Where' is an adverb, meaning in (or to) which place, direction or respect. 'Were' is a verb, the past tense of 'to be'. 'We're' is a contraction of 'we are'. For example:

Where are we going on holiday?

You were at home last night and now you are at work.

We're attending a training course today.

Your and you're

'Your' means belonging to you. 'You're' is the contraction of you are. For example:

> Your bag is in the other room.

> You're expected in half an hour.

Should, must and have to

'Should', 'must' and 'have to' are verbs that convey obligation. In writing, 'should' can be interpreted as weaker in meaning than 'must' or 'have to'. For example, if I write, 'You should always check your spelling before you send an e-mail' you might think I am just recommending this as good practice. You could see it as an option, not an obligation. On the other hand, if I write, 'You must always check your spelling before you send an e-mail', then I'm making it very clear that this is not an option; it is a directive. 'Have to' carries the same weight.

Without knowing your line of business, I can't usefully give more examples here – but you can see the potential problems. It's really worthwhile for you to formulate a list of words that may confuse colleagues or clients alike – and either avoid them or make sure you get them right!

Acronyms

Acronyms make an abbreviated word formed by the initial letters of other words or a compound noun. The idea is to make the subject easier to refer to and easier to remember.

When you use abbreviations and acronyms, write them in full at the first mention, then follow with the abbreviation in brackets: for example, Regional Development Agency (RDA). People tend not to do this when an acronym is very likely to be recognized internationally. An example would be the UN (United Nations). It does depend on your target audience. After that first explanation, you may just use the acronym in the text that follows.

I once received an e-mail referring to APAC populations. I imagined that the writer was referring to Asia Pacific populations... but decided to see if there were other acronyms for APAC. There certainly are! I will list just a few:

APAC: Asia and Pacific;

APAC: Asia Pacific Advisory Committee;

APAC: All People Are Customers;

APAC: Atlantic Pilotage Authority Canada.

Each group will no doubt have it that their target audience will, 100 per cent, understand their acronym. But my experience as a consultant tells me otherwise!

CASE STUDY   How an unexplained acronym created problems

A director was giving a presentation at a large multinational company recently. One slide, entitled 'BHAGs', was beamed across the hall and, without explaining the acronym, the director spoke enthusiastically on a ground-breaking vision for the company.

After a while, he asked if anyone had any questions. A hand went up, and one brave employee asked: 'What is a BHAG?' pronouncing the word as 'bag'.

'You don't know what a BEE-hag is?' asked the director, noticeably surprised. The questioner probably felt embarrassed. 'Would anyone like to explain?' continued the director. There was silence from the floor. It seemed that nobody could be actually sure what the acronym stood for. Certainly nobody volunteered to explain so it was likely that the questioner was not the only one not to understand.

For the record, BHAG (pronounced bee-hag) stands for 'Big, hairy, audacious goal'. It denotes a strategic and visionary statement that teams are likely to find emotionally compelling.

Would you agree the director made a key mistake here? His unexplained acronym became a business peril. If anyone didn't quite know what it meant, they either would have to:

- stick their neck out and ask its meaning; or
- remain in the dark because they didn't dare ask!

Even where you explain an acronym at the outset of a document, it helps to repeat the words in full from time to time. Have you noticed that although I explain the acronym 'non-NE' earlier in this book, I write it in full – 'non-native English' – on many occasions, to help reinforce it for you?

Active and passive

Most companies today favour the active over the passive voice in business writing, so it's good to understand the difference.

The active voice is where the subject does the action. Sentences that show this are:

The committee took action as a result.

The minute-taker handed the notes to the director.

The passive voice is where the subject of the active clause becomes secondary, where it is acted upon or receives the action. Often the word 'by' is added, as we can see in the following sentences:

Action was taken by the committee as a result.

The director was given the notes by the minute-taker.

In both these examples, we can still see the subjects (the committee and the minute-taker) but they are easier to see in the active sentences, as they appear first. That alone is why it's better practice to use the active voice in business writing. But there are other reasons why active writing is better. The following, very typical, example of passive writing in meetings notes demonstrates this: 'A decision was taken to take the matter further.'

When readers see a sentence such as this, they can be utterly confused. Who took the decision? In operational terms, what happens next? We can't know from the context. We need more information – yet experience shows people often don't go on to ask for that information.

Nominalization

Many business writers mistakenly think they must embellish or over-complicate their writing! Even the most effective speaker can seem to feel that to write simply and clearly is a sign of weakness.

Sometimes people can't break away from thinking that high word count and complex vocabulary signifies 'we're cleverer than you'. Historically, intellectual, academic writing, for example, uses nominalization, in which nouns are used in place of verbs. This may be useful in writing about concepts. But in business it can seem pompous and outdated. We saw in Chapter 5 how verbs can create vibrant content – but nominalizations do the complete opposite. These examples show the nominalization first, followed by the clearer verb form:

give clarification on this = clarify this;

in recognition of the fact = recognizing that;

during the installation process = when installing;

we are involved with negotiations = we are negotiating.

The verb form gives more energy: we know that something is happening in each case and that people are involved. With nominalization, users appear to hide behind language. That's rarely a great idea in business.

Your checklist for action

- When writing dates, times and measurements, one size doesn't fit all.

- Understand the conventions your readers use.

- If you don't do this, you may miss appointments, delivery deadlines, etc.

- Your order books may be adversely affected if you get dates, times and numbers wrong – your profits too.

- Write as precisely as possible to avoid misunderstandings: for example, 2nd January 2025.

- Don't assume readers know the common terms or abbreviations you use (particularly as your writing may be forwarded on to others). Write so that everyone will understand.

- Define the terms you will be using and check that your readers use the same ones.

- Make sure you write plain English, using words precisely.

- Use active rather than passive writing where appropriate.

- Look out for the common confusions described in this chapter. Make a note of others you come across – and ask colleagues to do the same.

11
Paper is here to stay

Although digital is undoubtedly in the ascendant when it comes to the written word, paper refuses to fade away, thanks to consumer support. We see books, leaflets, brochures, letters, reports and printouts continue to play an important role in the business world. In this arena we're seeing fairly traditional, emoji-free writing back in force.

As I write, Facebook has introduced a British-based quarterly print magazine, *Grow* (alongside an online version), to be available in 'selected airport and train business lounges' for readers in transit. They are doing this knowing that business leaders have limited time for long reads at work – and also knowing that there remains a need for in-depth articles for greater understanding of topics.

As an example in retail, Amazon in the US sent out printed toy catalogues for the first time in November 2018. Now that there are fewer physical stores, it's apparent that parents and their children often prefer to look through catalogues together, rather than browse online. It's a tactile experience that print can offer and effective writing underpinning alluring visuals can boost sales, especially in the run-up to lucrative seasonal festivities or birthdays.

Interestingly, there was an actual backlash when UK retailer Argos trialled catalogue-free stores, with many customers demanding they bring back paper brochures.

There's consistent feedback that:

- readers have greater recall of print over online messaging;
- they revisit it more often;
- when it comes to printed mailshots (validly sent to the target audience) readers can feel more valued by any offer you make – and trust the information more.

Although not strictly print as far as the end user is concerned, the fast-growing area of business audiobooks for on-the-go training, naturally does depend on the written word that scripts it.

CASE STUDY   Royal Mail UK

A Royal Mail UK study in 2015 identified that marketing mail still played an important role in today's rapidly transforming media landscape. New ways to create and enhance consumer relationships are evolving all the time, as is the ability to collect and analyse vast amounts of data on consumer behaviour.

They identified that what digital media hasn't changed is people:

We are still physical creatures that thrive on human contact and stimulation. Giving, receiving and handling tangible objects remain deep and intuitive parts of the human experience. In the never-ending stream of two-way virtual communication, sending a direct sensory experience of your brand can mark a pivotal moment in the customer journey.

The tips I have given you so far in the book will help here, as the writing system I teach works across all writing tasks. That said, I think it would help you to remember three particularly relevant points when it comes to writing for print:

1 Any mistakes you make are likely to be more apparent as readers have more time to focus on errors.

2 Any claims you make can be analysed with greater scrutiny when people have time to reflect on and revisit what you say.

3 If it's a stand-alone piece of writing, with no opportunity for an online, phone or face-to-face chat to clarify things, you can especially see why your words need to say what you mean them to say, in a way that's not open to misunderstanding.

Letters

Historically, business letters (now also referred to as 'snail mail') were a formal means of business communication sent by post or courier. In many cases they have either been replaced by informal social media interaction, as we've seen, or by e-mail (or as attachments to e-mail), all mainly for speed. Across the world though, we do still find plenty of occasions where people like or expect to receive a paper letter. This might be for a legal or financial matter, for orders, for apologies for something that's gone wrong, or an invitation of value and so on.

As you're seeing, you can (and must) innovate in business writing today and discard some of the things you may have been taught years ago. Yet there are still certain conventions to follow for your letters to achieve your objectives.

First of all, identify the purpose of your letter and its possible impact on your reader:

- Is it to inform? If so, why?

- Is it to instigate action? If so, what? Who by? How? When by?

- How do you want the reader to feel when reading your letter? Can your tone assist this?

Second, identify the format. Do you use templates and a standard font? Has this been assessed for readability? For example, Arial, Tahoma and Verdana (amongst others) can be more readable than some cursive fonts, especially for non-NE readers. How compatible is the font you use with other systems? Does the font size fall within the routinely used 10–15-point range? Many consider that 12 point offers optimum readability – though you still need to consider the needs of those with visual challenges and other needs, and adapt your writing accordingly.

Do you use a subject heading above your main text? Do you use a reference or code? An informative subject heading engages your reader's attention from the start. It also helps you identify the point of your letter. Customize it if you can. Even the use of the word 'your', as in 'Re: your contract XYZ', is more reader-friendly than 'Re: contract XYZ'. (Incidentally, you don't need to use 'Re:' at all; it's a question of house style.)

Third, identify how well your letters work. Ask yourself questions such as these each time:

- Did I achieve the right result from this letter?

- Or was there a problem? Why was that? Was it because of the English I used? What should I have written?

- Did I get no result when I had expected one? Why was that? Should I use English differently next time I write?

Traditional letter format

Here's an outline of a traditional letter format – but be mindful that even within the UK there are differing conventions as to where to place the date and address on a letter, and what salutations and endings to use, amongst other considerations. Other countries will naturally have differing conventions too. So once again, one size does not fit all and you would need to adapt the outline according to your chosen house style.

How to set out a business letter in English

Your company name and contact details
Addressee's name and job title
Addressee's company or organization name
Number or name of building
Name of street or road
Post town
Postcode (UK addresses)
County, district or state
Area code or zip code (US addresses)
Country

Date

Reference number

Opening salutation (with or without a comma, depending on house style)

Heading

Main body of text

Closing salutation (with or without a comma, depending on house style)

Name of writer
Position in organization

Enc. (refers to enclosures, if there are any)

Salutations

If you don't know the name of the person you're writing to, the opening salutation is generally 'Dear Sir or Madam' and the traditional closing salutation is 'Yours faithfully' according to UK English convention. In US English your letter could end with 'Sincerely' or 'Best regards' or 'Yours truly'.

If you know the person's name, use it in your opening salutation: for example, 'Dear Mr Smith' (or Mrs Smith, Ms Smith, Miss Smith). This is the formal use of their surname. Or you can write 'Dear Yusuf' (or Sara, etc); this is the informal use of their first name. When you end the letter, you write 'Yours sincerely' rather than 'Yours faithfully'.

Where possible, try to find out the name of the person to whom you are writing. Naturally, some situations will always stay formal, keeping to the 'Dear Sir or Madam' formula. But as relationship building can be crucial to business success today, it's really worthwhile personalizing your letter writing.

Open punctuation

You or your company choose whether you use open punctuation in business letters today. This simply means that you can have a comma after the opening salutation ('Dear ...'), or you can omit it. The same applies to your sign-off ('Yours ...'). Whichever option you choose, be consistent in both the salutation and the sign-off.

When flexibility is key, you need to adapt letter-writing templates

Although I've shown a standard format, effective business letter-writing is getting more creative. As circumstances change, we need to adapt each writing task. So when it comes to letter-writing you need to design templates that work for you and be prepared to change them as business expectations evolve. I'll shortly be showing you some creative sub-headings used effectively to illustrate what I mean.

First, be aware that although companies increasingly deal with customer complaints via social media rather than by letter (as we saw in Chapter 5), this still impacts on letter-writing style. It's confusing to have overly different writing styles within organizations. Look at this Tweet, sent by a train company to a customer (I've anonymized the details) who had tweeted to complain about a delayed train:

TranscountryRail (@TranscountryRail)

@mariexyz I can see you were 11 mins delayed into London Bridge, I do apologise for this Marie. Jon

We see the apology the complainant expects. But the language is still quite formal if we look at it alongside the language used by a fast food chain in reply to a complaint by a customer on Twitter (details anonymized) accompanied by a photo of a newly opened bag of crisps (a UK English word; 'chips' in US and other varieties of English):

Todxyz (@todxyz_)

Are you joking @fastfoodtogo? I was expecting a little more than that when I opened my bag of potato crisps #disappointing

FastFoodToGo (@fastfoodtogo)

@todxyz_ That does look a little stingy! Sorry, did you show our Team Members?

'Stingy' is a colloquial word for 'mean' and denotes 'under-filled' in this context. The informality of social media attunes readers to expect this type of conversational interaction – where companies aren't afraid to express empathy or say sorry where things go wrong.

If the vocabulary and tone in corporate letters is completely different from a company's social media voice, can you see how this can bewilder readers? It undermines brand consistency – and even credibility. You might 'like' and trust the company's social media voice and 'dislike', even mistrust, a 'formal' letter's distant tone.

Do any of these points strike a particular chord with you or your colleagues? They could make a springboard for wider discussion.

A letter that involves the reader with the company's narrative

You've seen the importance of storytelling in writing for social media and marketing in Chapter 5. We're seeing how an integrated approach to writing tasks can work wonders and as I mentioned earlier, creativity is needed in letter writing. The fixed templates of yesteryear rarely work.

So let me expand on the earlier case study in Chapter 4, on writing used at Nationwide. How do they use their compelling narrative in letters?

Let's take a look at extracts from one of their standard letters to illustrate what I mean. After their personalized, customer-centric heading, they mention:

> A warm welcome to your account... (details followed). Members such as yourself mean a lot to us – they make up the very fabric of who we are, and where we've come from.

They continue with sub-headings, which break what could have seemed a boring, technical letter into easy-to-read copy:

> **You can rest safe in the knowledge, we'll be looking after your savings**

Then they outline details of the account and what's involved, followed by the next sub-heading:

> **We're here to help**

Details follow of what they mean by this.

The letter ends:

> Thank you again for being a member of Nationwide. We were founded when a group of people came together to help each other buy houses, save and generally get more out of their money – and we appreciate you being part of that story, and helping us continue to grow.

Note the inclusive language: it brings the recipient into their continuing story and thanks them for their valued participation.

The message aligned with their television and online advertising campaign at that time. This level of cohesive communication assists the authenticity of their story and helps engagement in the narrative. It's yet another example of effective business writing and it can be a joy to design!

Even as a start-up you can design simple letters that impress, as this letter shows:

Dear Mrs Talbot

How can I help?

We value our customers and we make it our duty to understand their needs and requirements so that we can help them to make their businesses work even better.

Can we do that for you?

Investing a small amount of your valuable time in a brief appointment is all that I ask of you to enable me to understand your business needs, and offer you helpful suggestions as to how you could reduce costs, at the same time as taking your business forward.

Yours sincerely
Signature and company name

The simplicity of the message and the development of a two-way relationship (between me and them) made an impact. This agency achieved this by using creative sub-headings and by writing 'I', 'we' and 'you' – and yes, it worked: I bought from them.

This two-way dynamic is becoming more expected in letters that were previously jargon-riddled and convoluted in certain professions. This has been picked up, as I write, by the Academy of Medical Royal Colleges in the UK where outpatient letters are the most-written letters sent in the National Health Service. In their guidance 'Please, write to me' the Academy go so far as to say doctors have to learn a new skill: writing letters directly to patients in plain English that's well-structured, informative, useful, supportive and engaging.

This is quite a breakthrough and maybe you can think of other professions that would do well to take note.

Specific tips about addressing letters

Always check the spelling of the name of the person you're writing to and their correct job title. Readers can be quickly offended when their personal details are incorrect. There may also be commercial implications if compliance-related documentation has wrong details.

It can be difficult, though, if you don't know which gender a foreign or unfamiliar name relates to. Ideally, make enquiries; maybe someone else will know. Or you could use the person's full name at the beginning of the letter – for example, 'Dear Chris Palmer' – to avoid embarrassment or offence.

CVs/résumés and cover letters

Do have a regularly updated CV (also called résumé) as a written overview of your job experience and qualifications, even if you're not applying for another job. It helps you identify milestones you've achieved, the skills you're developing and the personal attributes you have enhanced. It also helps you express 'your brand': what makes you special over and above the next person.

Most CVs are e-mailed to prospective employers, so once again it's your writing that's judged initially. With stiff competition for jobs, employers can hit hard, often ditching CVs with mistakes or that fail to answer the brief or impress.

Employers see a CV as an applicant's 'sales document'. The most articulate speaker in the world might not get to interview stage, simply because his or her written words are the weak link. So choose words that describe the skills you can bring to the company. Why are you the perfect fit? Research the company and tailor your writing if you want to get the job.

Professional social networking site LinkedIn (amongst others), provides great advice and even CV templates to customize for 'brand you'. They show the current way of doing things, as approaches change. Year on year, they list what they term CV 'buzzwords' that have become clichés through over-use, such as: creative, results-oriented, motivated, responsible and so on. None of them are 'bad' words but if everyone uses them, you won't make your mark.

Showcase how good and impactful your writing style is, and identify the words that list your skills, show your talents for solving problems, improving efficiency, developing relationships, etc.

Take time to make your CV 'look good', using all the tips on word power and layout that you've been learning in the word power skills writing system. Provide links to your online activity.

Remember employers will check your posts and it's in your interests to show them a professional personal brand that will boost your employability. So don't post inappropriate information or discriminatory comments. Reputation matters as much for you as for any company that takes you on.

Include only facts that are true and accurately describe your personal attributes. You must be able to deliver what you say you can.

Cover letter with CV

Some employers like a good covering letter (or e-mail) with your CV. Use it to improve your chances of getting to interview stage. Customize it and send it with your CV to the correct person, spelling their details and job title correctly, and to the right address.

Do:

- Show you've done some research on the company and refer to something relevant on its website, such as its values and goals, expressing how yours align.

- Answer the question 'Why should you get the job?' by highlighting the special skills you can bring.

- Think of your potential employer (and their likely customers and suppliers), as much as yourself when you write. You've got to persuade and build bridges to get that job!

- Make sure 'brand you' shines out, to set you apart positively from the rest.

- Show what you expect from a prospective employer as much as what they can expect from you.

- State your availability.

- Run a final spellcheck and grammar check; after all, if English is required in the job, make sure yours is perfect in your application! Ask someone's advice if necessary.

Depending on culture and personality, people tend even in their native language either to understate their suitability for any vacancy being advertised or in some cases to over-embellish it. The following non-native English writers' descriptions of their suitability as job candidates definitely fall into the second category:

An accountant: 'I dispose of untouchable integrity and corresponding success and my brilliance is impressive.'

A marketing manager: 'My knowledge, ratio and outstanding attributions decide that my future will be with your company.'

These are examples of what I term 'over-Englishing': the desire to outdo native English writers with an exaggerated use of language that deviates from the original. It is in essence an imaginary language – and in the ultimate analysis, it has no meaning! I could rewrite what I think they mean to say (and this isn't at all clear, probably not even in their own minds) as follows:

> An accountant: 'A successful professional with integrity, I will be pleased to use my expertise in the post advertised.'
>
> A marketing manager: 'I am looking to take my career to the next level and have every confidence that my excellent credentials, expert knowledge and skills base will deliver what you seek in this post.'

Your checklist for action

- Realize that printed material may be scrutinized more and recall may be higher: this also means that mistakes and flawed logic may be spotted more easily.

- Know what you want your written piece to achieve; enable the result you need.

- Check that the look and feel of your writing aligns with values shown in other corporate communication. Cohesive writing has authenticity.

- In letters, write your recipient's personal details correctly; use the correct salutation and sign-off; build in rapport and politeness and consider creative sub-headings to engage.

- Always remember that it's a person or people you are writing to – and use plain English.

- Represent yourself, your personal brand and your company well.

- Don't make assumptions; write to your brief and for readers' needs. Answer any questions systematically.

- Don't over-complicate your writing, don't use clichés or make false claims.

- Design a CV/résumé that's a 'sales document' for 'brand you' showing writing skills that give you the competitive edge in the information age.

Conclusion
What will you do differently – and better?

As I write, Jeff Weiner, CEO of the world's largest professional-networking site, LinkedIn, says most employers list soft skills (and most tellingly, written communication skills feature at the forefront of these) as the ones they value most.

Alongside these, employers also seek coding skills which, interestingly, also depend on writing unambiguous messages in plain language, for today's and tomorrow's workplace.

This book has given you a wealth of advice to help you build knowledge and confidence in these areas.

Now it's over to you

With fresh eyes, think about how you've closed the skills gap between where you were when you started the book – and where you are now. Then don't stop there! Make improvements so you get to where you want to be.

Enjoy using the #wordpowerskills system to help you create a great 'reader experience' – across all sectors, cultures and generations you encounter.

Which tips particularly help you? Jot them down and chart your progress over the coming months. Make your mark by sharing findings with others.

You see, that's what this book has given me the opportunity to do. I've shared findings from the hundreds of workshops and coaching sessions I've delivered. It's how we learn the business

English that our readers expect. The channels and language variety may change, but the principles of writing excellent professional communication are constant.

Your take-away message – be clear and professional, be passionate and entice buy-in!

Understand how crucial it is to tailor your business writing for your target readership at any given time. Clarity matters. Relevance matters. Vitality really matters too. Why choose dull words that can make you or your brand seem bored and boring? How much better to use words as a springboard for personal and organizational success by injecting the right word power! I've been enthused at helping clients write gas safety handbooks or instructions on how to lay underwater cables, simply because their enthusiasm has been infectious. They've been as passionate about getting their words right as, say, the dedicated marketing and sales professionals that I've also been delighted to train.

For me, the most important thing now is to help *you* communicate effectively, professionally and respectfully. If you change anything at all for the better as a result of this workplace primer, you'll not only make me a very happy author – you'll also boost your employability throughout your career!